HARVESTING OUR TEARS

Susan Blum Gerding, Ed.D.

Boca Raton, Florida

Harvesting Our Tears

A Process for Grieving Our Loved Ones
Susan Blum Gerding, Ed.D.

Music Composed by Fredrick P. Schott
Performed by *Anawim* , the music ministry of the
Basilica Cathedral of Covington, Kentucky

English translation of the *Catechism of the Catholic Church* for the United States of America Copyright © 1994, United States Catholic Conference, Inc.-- Libreria Editrice Vaticana. English translation of the: Catechism of the Catholic Church Modifications from the Editio Typica Copyright © 1997, United States Catholic Conference, Inc.--Libreria Editrice Vaticana. Used with permission.

Scripture (with exception of those verses on first page of each session) taken from the HOLY BIBLE NEW INTERNATIONAL VERSION, Copyright © 1973, 1978, 1984 by International Bible Society. Used by permission of Zondervan Publishing House. All rights reserved. (Verses on first pages of each session from a variety of sources dependent upon the composer of the music.)

Passages from *When Bad Things Happen to Good People* by Harold S. Kushner used with permission from the publisher, HarperCollins, 1981. All rights reserved.

Copyright (C) 2000 From *Men Don't Cry: Women Do* by Terry Martin and Kenneth Doka. Reproduced by permission of Routledge/Taylor & Francis Books, Inc.

Passages from*The Death of a Child* by Elaine Stillwell used with permission of the author.

Illustrations by Judd A. Heicklen

ISBN:1-883520-26-6
Library of Congress Control Number: 2004096833

Jeremiah Press
5840 Wind Drift Lane
Boca Raton, Florida 33433
Fax: 561-368-2322
JeremiahPr@aol.com
www.JeremiahPress.com

Dedicated with Everlasting Love
to
Daniel Howard Blum
November 19, 1969 - December 25, 1994
and
Debora Elizabeth Blum Maners
October 5, 1964 - January 5, 2004

About The Author

A veteran Catholic lay evangelizer, Dr. Susan Blum Gerding has been actively proclaiming the Good News since 1979, but this is her first foray into the field of bereavement ministry. Sue experienced the sudden death of her youngest of four children, Danny, 25, when a drunk driver plowed through a red light at 80 mph on Christmas Day, 1994, killing Danny instantly. Tragedy struck again when her oldest child Debbie, 39, married less than two years and with a five month old daughter, was diagnosed with Stage IV Lung Cancer which had spread to her lymph glands, bones, and brain. A lifelong nonsmoker, Debbie fought a courageous battle until her death exactly eight weeks later on January 5, 2004. Failing to find a Catholic faith-based, structured support group to attend, Sue embarked on the challenge of designing "Harvesting Our Tears" which could be used by individuals or in groups in the 19,000 Catholic parishes in the United States.

A convert to the Roman Catholic faith, Sue received her master's degree in Pastoral Ministry from St. Thomas University, Miami, and her doctorate in Adult Education/ Leadership Development at Florida Atlantic University. She was the founding editor of *The Catholic Evangelist* magazine and has written a total of eleven books and evangelization training manuals, including the *1993 Text, Study, Guide, and Implementation Process for Go and Make Disciples* developed in consultation with the NCCB Committee on Evangelization.

Her very first book, *The Ministry of Evangelization* was published by Liturgical Press, Collegeville, MN and is still in print. Recently, *Lay Ministers, Lay Disciples: Evangelizing Power in the Parish,* co-authored with Rev. Frank DeSiano, CSP, was published by Paulist Press (1999). *Christ the Cornerstone: Christians Coping in a World of Chaos and Confusion* (2002) and *Called and Sent: Living the Eucharist* (2002) are her two most recent books.

She is the founding president of Isaiah Ministries, Inc., which has offered a model of clergy/lay preaching teams and local parish involvement in Isaiah Parish Missions throughout the United States, Canada, and Europe since 1984. A popular speaker at national, diocesan, and parish conferences throughout the U.S., she is also the president of Jeremiah Press, which specializes in publishing books on Catholic spirituality.

In 1984, she was awarded the *Pro Ecclesia et Pontifice Medal* conferred by Pope John Paul II and the *National Lay Evangelizer of the Year* award, conferred by the Paulist National Catholic Evangelization Association. In 1996, she received the *Pope Paul VI Award for Leadership in Catholic Evangelization*, given by the National Council for Catholic Evangelization.

Sue lives with her husband Ed in Boca Raton, Florida, where they are active members of St. Jude Church. Together, they are the parents of ten children and sixteen grandchildren. Since the death of her children, Sue has studied extensively in the field of bereavement ministry and grief management and is a Certified Minister of Consolation (National Catholic Bereavement Ministry.)

"Harvesting Our Tears" is a contribution to the field of bereavement ministry in the Catholic faith tradition with the two-fold purpose of 1) assuring those who mourn the presence and comfort of a living, energetic, viable "God among us" and 2) as a memorial to her two beloved children, Danny and Debbie, and all children who have died before their time.

CONTENTS

God of Life,
There are days when the burdens we carry chafe our
shoulders and wear us down,
when the road seems dreary and endless,
the skies gray and threatening,
when our lives have no music in them,
and our hearts are lonely,
and our souls have lost their courage.

Flood the path with light, we beseech thee, Lord.
Turn our eyes to where the Heavens are full of promise.
Amen.

. . . St. Augustine

Welcome to the *Harvesting Our Tears Grieving Process.* These sessions are designed to help assist and guide you during your own process of mourning the loss of your loved one. Each person's losses are unique, and each person's grief is different. However, almost everyone has one thing in common: TEARS.

Tears have the uncanny ability to express both extreme sorrow and intense joy. Hopefully, our tears will help us bridge that terrible gap between the sorrow surrounding our loss and the hope of a renewed sense of joy.

We are using the imagery of "gathering" or "harvesting" our tears as opposed to "wasting" or "ignoring" all of these tears.

The underlying thesis is that the tears, as well as grief, itself, are positive and helpful factors in our recovery from the loss of a loved one. If we can imagine our tears as raindrops, watering the scorched earth of sorrow and pain, we can see our tears nurturing and nourishing recovery and growth.

In my own support group, we joked, "If we could collect all of our tears, we would be able to eliminate the drought in the entire state." We all wondered how we could shed such copious tears -- "Where did they all come from?" . . . and "Why aren't we investing in Kleenex?"

Well, we will not be collecting our tears literally, but we do want to view them positively, as a means of transforming our pain into peace. Perhaps we can use the acrostic for TEARS as a reminder of the role our tears play: "Trust , Expect, Allow, Remember, Share."

Symbolism

Our tears are symbolized by the clear pitcher of water on the table before you, and the plants represent your loved ones during their lifetime -- fully alive, vibrant. During these next eight weeks, the large plant will change, symbolizing the Paschal mystery of our lives.

All faiths and denominations are welcome in *Harvesting Our Tears,* but the process will incorporate the nature, substance, and experience of the Catholic faith.

The format for each session includes scripture, prayer, and a musical meditation, at the beginning of each session. The songs are original compositions by Fred Schott, mostly written when he was in the seminary, and performed by *Anawim,* the music ministry at the Basilica Cathedral of Covington, Ky.

Sharing Your Stories

The bulk of each session and the most important part is the time you spend either sharing your own stories or listening to each other's stories in complete confidentiality. *Harvesting Our Tears* is not group psychotherapy and it is not designed to "fix" or resolve issues. It will enable you to share your thoughts, concerns, and feelings in a safe environment, knowing that you are well loved by God, and, as bonding occurs among you, by each other.

TEARS

Trust that tears are good for you.

Expect them. Tears are unpredictable and often uncontrollable.

Allow your tears to flow freely.

Remember fondly with your tears.

Share your tears with the whole world by transforming them.

Dual Responsibility

As a participant in the group, you have a dual responsibility:

1) to talk about your own experience, and

2) to listen to others'.

The key to recovery from grief is your ability to talk about your loved one, the circumstance of the death, your feelings of sadness, confusion, loss, abandonment, anger or whatever your true feelings are. Remember, feelings are neither right nor wrong; they just are!

It also must be noted here that not everyone weeps copious amounts of tears; some do not weep at all, except during the initial stages of their grief process. We will learn that there are many different ways to grieve, but for most people, the most important one is telling your story over and over until there is no urgent need to tell it again.

If the key to healing is talking, the keystone is a rock-solid foundation of confidentiality. It must be understood by everyone that nothing leaves the room which assures all of us that our privacy will be respected. Also, each person must listen non-judgmentally, neither attempting to resolve issues, nor giving advice. This is not a time for deep or extended discussions; nor is it a forum for other agendas. Listed here are a few guidelines for small group discussions. It is important that everyone agrees to these.

Origins

Let me share how this grieving process came into existence. When I searched for a Catholic support group that would fulfill my yearning for understanding my grief, for providing theological and pastoral support, and for fostering healing, I could not find one that was structured, limited in size, and close-ended. That is to say, not a "drop-in" group of people who have been meeting for years and years.

Unable to find such a Catholic faith-based group, I accepted a friend's invitation to attend one at her local Presbyterian church. *Walking the Mourner's Path* is a national, nondenominational program founded by the Episcopal Church. The process is excellent and I recommend it highly. *www. mournerspath.com.*

However, I soon realized the potential value of such a program for the Catholic Church, utilizing not only scripture and prayer, but the richness and fullness of sacrament, tradition, theology, imagery, music, ritual, catechesis, and community.

The Spirit began working overtime within me. For the first time in months, I allowed myself to feel the surge of creativity within me as part of my own healing process.

So, let's get down to the heart of the matter now . . . my broken heart, your broken heart, and the broken hearts of millions of people who are mourning the unexplainable or explainable, unexpected or expected deaths of their spouses, children, parents, siblings, and friends.

Note: This manual can be used by individuals not in a group. In this case, please take care to do all of the homework assignments and journaling. Share your responses to the questions with a trusted friend.

Group Guidelines

1. **listen respectfully**
2. **everyone speaks**
3. **participate fully**
4. **maintain confidentiality**
5. **no side conversations**
6. **no interruptions**
7. **no trying to "fix"**
8. **attend all meetings**
9. **no hidden agenda**

Session One
ACQUAINTED WITH GRIEF

Introductions

Prayer: + In the name of the Father and of the Son and of the Holy Spirit. Gracious God, Comforter of those who Mourn, we thank you and praise you for all the goodness in our lives. Send your Holy Spirit to be with us as we seek your healing, as we share our own painful stories, and as we make new friends in this group.   Thank you for the promise of everlasting life through the suffering, death, and resurrection of your own beloved son, Jesus Christ, our lord and redeemer now and forever. Amen

Scripture: I Corinthians 13: 4 - 8
Love is patient; love is kind. Love is not jealous, it does not put on airs, it is not snobbish. Love is never rude, it is not self seeking; it is not prone to anger, neither does it brood over injuries. Love does not rejoice in what is wrong but rejoices with the truth. There is no limit to love's forbearance, to its trust, its hope, its power to endure. Love never fails.

Hymn Meditation:
"Love Never Fails"
(For My Parents)

Love never fails . . .There is no limit
To its trust, its hope, ability to heal.
Love Never Fails.

Love is patient, love is kind, never selfish, never rude.
Love delights in the truth, is ready to forgive, endures whatever comes.

As the Father has loved me, so I have loved you. This is my command to you: have love within your heart and I will live in you.

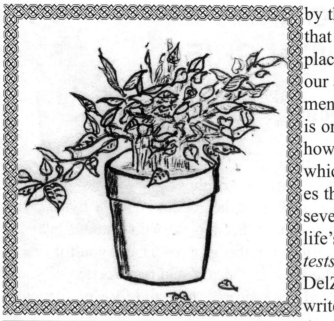

Symbol of Life: *The living plants represent the life of your loved ones in their prime . . . vibrant, healthy, thriving. It may be difficult to remember them this way now, but this is how they would want you to remember them.*

What is Grief?

Most experts in the field of bereavement typically describe grief as the process by which we adapt to a loss. However, Dr. Patrick M. DelZoppo, a clinical thanatologist and a national leader in Bereavement Ministry, described grief more dramatically in his book, *Mourning: The Journey from Grief to Healing.* "Grief is the *protest* of our body, mind, and spirit to the loss we have experienced, the severity of which will be determined by the value that we have placed upon our attachment. There is one loss, however, which causes the most severe of life's *protests,*" DelZoppo writes, " the death of one whom we have loved. It is in the irreversibility of that final loss that the protest of grief causes the greatest separation pain.

"In grief," he continues, "a God who created life comes to our aid again, not to spare us from the effects of grief and the pain of separation that are absolutely necessary but to bring us to another spiritual level through a process which we call mourning.

"Mourning is the prerequisite for healing. In fact, mourning itself is actually the beginning of a critical journey where grief is acknowledged, felt, understood and expressed. To mourn is to feel the loss at every level of our existence. Is it frightening? Yes," DelZoppo concludes, "But to mourn means that we are fully alive."

Grief as Protest

I resonate with this particular definition, of grief as *protest*, for our bodies, minds, and spirits truly *protest* the terrible

Grief is . . .

. . . a "protest" to loss
. . . a normal response to loss
. . . a natural part of life
. . . an individual journey
. . . a process
. . . multi-faceted
. . . painful
. . . exhausting
. . . temporary
. . . yours alone
. . . "all about you"

9

loss of a loved one. We protest the loss; we fight back against the loss; we refuse to let our loved one "go quietly into the night." We do not want to be a widow or widower; we do not want to be an "adult orphan;" we do not want to be the "only sibling left."

Especially when the death is not expected, everything within us cries out, "No!" "Impossible!" "Not fair!" "Surreal!" We cry such an enormous amount of tears that we are surpised to know our tear ducts are even capable of producing that many. We flinch and hide in our bedrooms; we isolate ourselves after all the guests go home; we exhaust ourselves, busy with mundane distractions.

Our hearts rip in half; our minds go crazy; and our spirits tumble, a whirlwind of confusion. Sometimes we give up, totally exhausted and confused by our inability to get a grip on life again, to 'pull ourselves up by our bootstraps,' and, in extreme cases, we die unless intervention occurs.

Grief doesn't wait. "Protest" doesn't wait. It is here. And it needs to be dealt with, one way or another. You cannot go around grief, or under grief, or over it. The only way to go *through grief* is to go *through grief.*

Grief is a protest which must be recognized, faced, experienced, overcome, and resolved. Facing into that protest, going through it, is called grieving or mourning. Because grief is so painful, it is often viewed as completely negative. But, actually, grief is a very positive and psychologically healthy state, even though painful. Grief allows us to resolve many issues. It also marks us as human.

Grief is not...

. . . a choice you make

. . . an option

. . . a disease

. . . an emotion

. . . something you "just get over"

. . . "healed by time"

It is necessary to immerse ourselves in the pain of grief to heal from it, no matter what our grieving pattern is. It is like an infection which must be lanced: severe pain precedes the healing. But the pain must be there to recognize the need for healing.

Some experts in the field use the analogy that grief is like a third-degree burn . . . extremely painful and long healing. But, like the burn, healing must occur or infection and disease will occur. Scars will remain.

Adjustment

Harvesting Our Tears is a process designed, not to eliminate or negate the pain or confusion of grief, but to guide the process of mourning and transform the grief from subconscious violence against ourselves to the intentional, peaceful acceptance of a new, possibly even joyful, way of life.

Four Tasks of Mourning

1. To accept the reality of the loss.
2. To experience the pain of grief.
3. To adjust to an environment in which the deceased is missing.
4. To "emotionally relocate" the deceased and move on with life.

William Worden, Ph.D., *Grief Counseling and Grief Therapy*

A Word About Journaling

Sr. Mauryeen O'Brien writes in *The New Day Journal, A Journey from Grief to Healing,* "Writing in a journal is a good way to discover and articulate what you are going through . . . Journal keeping can also be a form of prayer. . . . Journaling allows you to get an overall picture of yourself, your rhythms, your direction, and your insights into the specific events of your daily existence and their accompanying emotions. Articulating this story of what has happened to you since -- and because of -- the loss of your loved one is a vital tool in moving yourself to the point where you can begin to heal."*

One of the greatest values of a journal is to be able to look back at it after a period of time to see what you had written in the early days of grief. Sometimes, one finds the only words you were able to write . . . "Angry! Angry! Angry!" or something similar. Do not be concerned about spelling or grammar, just jot down whatever you are feeling, thinking, doing."

(* Used with permission Copyright ACTA Publications (800)-397-2282, www.actapublications.com)

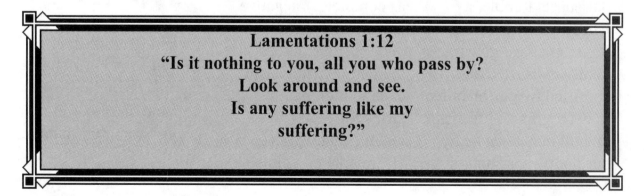

Lamentations 1:12
"Is it nothing to you, all you who pass by?
Look around and see.
Is any suffering like my
suffering?"

Your Story

1. Tell us a little about you and your background. How long have you lived here? Occupation/Retired? Family?

_____

_____

_____

_____

2. Who is your loved one that you lost? What were the circumstances of the death? Sudden or expected? Accident or illness?

_____

_____

_____

_____

3. How long ago was the death? If an illness, how long from the diagnosis to the death?

_____

_____

_____

_____

_____

4. Tell us what your life is like now.

_____

_____

_____

_____

_____

Ponderings . . .

What does the Church say about death? "The Christian meaning of death is revealed in the light of the *Paschal mystery* of the death and resurrection of Christ in whom resides our only hope. The Christian who dies in Christ Jesus is 'away from the body and at home with the Lord' "(*2 Cor 5:8*) *Catechism of the Catholic Church (cited hereafter as CCC) #1681.*

Supportive Scripture: "I am the resurrection and the life. He who believes in me will live, even though he dies, and whoever lives and believes in me will never die. Do you believe this?" (*John 11:26*).

Practical Suggestions:
1. Make a list of things that **absolutely must be done**, and then ask as many people as possible to help you do them.
2. Do not make major decisions now.
3. Wear favorite articles of clothing of your loved one for comfort.

Prayerful Suggestions:
1. Take quiet time for prayer, meditation, and reflection. If you feel you cannot pray, perhaps prayerful music from the "Harvesting Our Tears" CD will help you relax with God.

Food for Thought: "But tell not Misery's son that life is fair." *H. K. White*

Homework: Please bring a few of your favorite photos of your loved one to the session next week. *Option:* Also, if you are interested, please complete the Grief Pattern Inventory in Appendix A, including your score, for next week.

Serenity Prayer
God, grant me the serenity to accept the things
I cannot change,
the courage to change the things I can,
and the wisdom to know the difference. Amen.

Journaling

Date: _____

1. A significant event that occurred this week.
2. The person who was most important to me this week.
3. Changes I observe happening to me.
4. My plans for next week include . . .
5. Notes to myself . . .

_____

_____

_____

_____

_____

_____

_____

_____

_____

_____

_____

_____

_____

_____

_____

_____

_____

_____

_____

_____

_____

_____

_____

_____

_____

_____

_____

_____

Session Two
MY BELOVED

Prayer: +In the name of the Father and of the Son and of the Holy Spirit. Heavenly Father, we thank you and praise you for creating each one of us so differently. Our emotions, minds, behaviors, thoughts, and yearnings are each so unique. Help us to realize the differences in the way that we grieve together, always as your sons and daughters. Be with us as we continue on our journey of mourning. Give us the strength and courage to face into our losses, to work through our grief, and someday to find peace and happiness once again. All of this we pray in Jesus's Most Holy Name. Amen.

Scripture: "How beautiful is your love, my sister, my bride,
how much more delightful is your love than wine,
and the fragrance of your ointments than all spices!"

(Song of Songs 4:10)

Hymn Meditation:

"My Beloved"
(For all who have ever loved dearly)

I am to my beloved as my beloved is to me.
With you I rejoice and am glad, for our love is more precious than wine.
Our love is more precious than wine.

Arise my love, my beloved, and see that the winter is past.
Let me see your face and hear your sweet voice,
for my lover belongs to me, and I to him (her.)

The flowers bloom full in the meadow, and the song of the dove is heard.
Set me as a seal, a seal upon your heart,
for my lover belongs to me, and I to her (him).

very close friends with whom you can talk over your thoughts and feelings.

Just verbalizing a thought or feeling outloud helps. "I will never see little Sammy play baseball again," or "I will never go on a cruise with Frank again." It's called "counting your losses." The antidote is "counting your blessings," and at this point of transition in the grief process, it is extremely important that you do both.

In his book, *Your Healing Journey Through Grief,* Stanley Cornils (founder of Grief Recovery Seminars) lists several benefits of talking:

Symbol of Life: The lush, green plants, the symbol of our loved ones, represent their vitality. We shared our tears with them in life. We share our tears with them now.

Sharing Our Stories

One of the best activities you can choose during this time is talking. Talking to your friends, your relatives, your close family members, your co-workers. Talk, and talk, and talk!

After a while, when you have felt like talking to everyone, including the librarian and the postman (which, by the way, is called "syndicating our sorrows,") ideally you will find a few

The Value of Talking

1. Talking about our sorrow helps release tension and dissolve the pain of the grief experience. Each time we talk about a painful experience, our pain is eased just a little more.

2. Talking has a therapeutic value. First, it is cathartic. Through verbalization, our feelings of loss, loneliness, guilt, anger, and hostility are brought to the surface of our consciousness where we can deal with them.

3. Talking provides us with insight, which enables us to see more clearly our real feelings and problems.

4. Finally, the talking process establishes a wholesome relationship with the person in whom we confide.

Grieving: A Choice

The grieving process offers us a choice: to live again or to wallow in mere lifeless existence. We can choose to waste our tears, allowing them

My Beloved Danny

to simply go down the drain or sink into the grave, or we can symbolically collect our tears, gather them, harvest them for nourishment and refreshment. God tells us, "I will change your tears into laughter!" ("But not right away," I warn.)

Part of My Story

Yes, mourning gives us a choice: life or death. I know. When death comes to a child, intense grieving occurs. My youngest child, Danny, 25, was killed instantly on Christmas Day, 1994, when a drunk driver plowed through a red light at 80 mph.

Several months later, after I spoke of Danny's death while presenting an Isaiah Parish Mission, a woman rushed up to me and said, "Oh, I know exactly how you feel! My whole life has fallen apart! I cry and cry all day long--at every moment, it seems. I can't even go back to work yet with such intense grief. The only comfort I have is my daily visit to my daughter's grave!"

I identified with some of what she said until I asked her when her daughter had died. "Fourteen years ago this month," she replied.

"Fourteen years?" I incredulously thought to myself and decided on the spot that I had a decision to make. I chose right then and there not to allow myself the debilitating luxury of years and years of grief.

> "The most important thing I can tell any grieving person is that this terrible, horrible, "death -to-the-soul" pain that we feel . . . will go away eventually."

Another Part of My Story

Grieving is a luxury when it moves from grief to self-pity. How do I know this? Because I am an expert at both.   Nine years after Danny's death, I buried my oldest child, Debbie, a lifelong nonsmoker,

My Beloved Debbie

after a courageous eight-week battle with lung cancer. Debbie had been married less than two years and left a young husband and a seven- month old baby daughter. I am an expert at grieving and at wallowing, especially with the death of this second precious child; but more importantly, I am becoming an expert at recovery, a "scarred and wounded expert" but, nevertheless, an expert.

The most important thing I can tell any grieving person is that this terrible, horrible, "death -to-the-soul" pain that we feel, these gallons of tears that we weep, the bottomless depth of our loss, the helplessness, the fury, the disappointment, the disillusionment . . . whatever we are feeling . . . will go away eventually.

Right now, you may not think that the pain will ever end. But, it will.

Trust me. I know. We never forget our loved ones -- whether they are our children, or spouses, or parents, or siblings, or friends -- and the impact of their deaths leave us scarred and shaken, never to be the same . . . but the excruciating "worst pain in our lives" does go away. I promise that you will feel better! Be assured that you will find relief.

However, time alone will not heal the wounds of grief. "The secret of being lifted up through grief is to be fully engaged in the mourning process," Dr. Patrick Del Zoppo, writes in his book *Mourning: The Journey from Grief to Healing.* "Understanding your loss requires an ongoing review of what happened to you along the way." Now it's time for "Your Story" and pictures of your beloved.

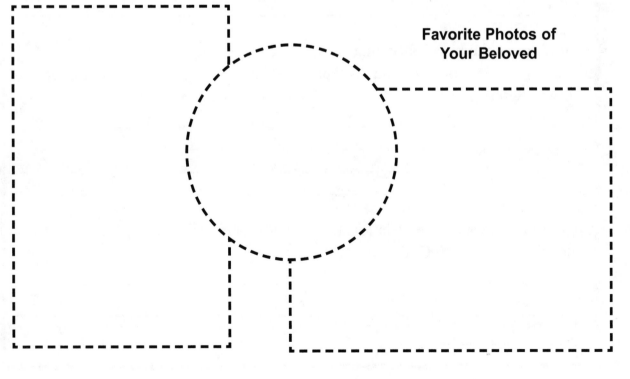

Favorite Photos of Your Beloved

Your Story

1. Show the pictures of your beloved that you brought with you today and share with the group what occasions they represent. Tell us about him or her. What were they like?

_____
_____
_____
_____

2. Share one of the happiest times you ever had with your beloved.

_____
_____
_____
_____

3.   Think about the words of the song, "My Beloved." How do they apply to you and your beloved?

_____
_____
_____
_____

4. Reflect on the possibility that those lines were written to express the relationship between you and God, as well. What does that say about your relationship with God?

_____
_____
_____
_____

5. What qualities of your relationship with your beloved do you find also in your relationship with God?

_____
_____
_____

Ponderings . . .

What does the Church say about the unity of love?
"One cannot honor another person without blessing God his Creator. One cannot adore God without loving all men, his creatures. The Decalogue brings man's religious and social life into unity"*(CCC #2069).*

Supportive Scriptures: "As the Father has loved me, so have I loved you. Now remain in my love" *(John 15: 9).*

"My command is this: Love each other as I have loved you" *(John 15: 12).*

Practical Suggestions:
1. Look through photo albums and discover more photos of your loved one. Remember and honor those memories.

2. Think of other people who also loved your beloved. Ask them what their favorite memories are.

3. **Don't** sell the house, move or make major decisions for at least a year. **Do** consider your options, plan ahead and seek advice.

Prayerful Suggestions:
1. Pray the Glorious Mysteries of the Rosary and think how God rejoiced (danced) on the day that your beloved was born.

2. Start a "Gratitude List." At the back of this workbook you will find a "Gratitude List." Write down five things you are grateful for. (They don't have to be the five things you are *most* grateful for, just grateful.) You will be adding to this list every week.

Food for Thought:
"Often the test of courage is not to die but to live." *Alfieri*

"The crosses which we make for ourselves by a restless anxiety as to the future are not crosses which come from God." *(Anon)*

Journaling

1. *A significant event that occurred this week.*
2. *The person who was most important to me this week.*
3. *Changes I observe happening to me.*
4. *My plans for next week include . . .*
5. *Notes to myself . . .*

_____

_____

_____

_____

_____

_____

_____

_____

_____

_____

_____

_____

_____

_____

_____

_____

_____

_____

_____

_____

_____

_____

_____

_____

Session III
SUFFERING AND HOPE

Prayer: +In the name of the Father and of the Son and of the Holy Spirit. Amen. God of Wisdom, God of Light, we come before your throne with grieving hearts and tearful eyes. We ache from wondering about our loved one's death. We hold so many conflicting emotions, and we can't even think straight sometimes. Please help us to accept the mystery of our loss. Send us peace, understanding and hope in the midst of our confusion and pain. Help us believe always your promise for a future full of hope. Amen.

Scripture: "For I know well the plans I have in mind for you, says the LORD,
plans for your welfare, not for woe!
Plans to give you a future full of hope."
Jeremiah 29: 11

Hymn Meditation:

"A Future Full of Hope"
(For Sue Blum)

Refrain--**I know well the plans I have for you,
plans for your welfare not for woe,
Plans to give you a future, a future full of hope.**

**You are my people, I am your God. When you pray and trust in me
with all your heart and soul, I will answer you.**

**I will show you kindness and faithfulness. I have loved you with all of my
heart, with a love that has no end. Forever you are mine.**

**I will lead you safely from all your foes. You shall come home singing songs
of joy for the goodness of the Lord. You shall weep no more.**

**I will make a new covenant with the house of Israel.
I will write it on their heart of stone. You are my people, I am your God.**

22

Death

Death is a normal part of life. We all know that, but it surely does not feel normal when it happens to us, to our family, to our loved ones. Death is about as abnormal an event in my life as anything else I can think of. Death takes life, the life of a loved one, and our life stops. Time stops as we freeze in numbness or disbelief. Even if the death is expected, when it happens, it happens! It is so final.

The Judeo-Christian tradition is unmistakably pro-grief, pro-tears. When Israelites of old suffered a great loss, they donned sackcloth and ashes. They ripped their garments, usually over their hearts, the tear in the cloth symbolizing a scar on the soul that can never be repaired. They designated a wall in Jerusalem the Wailing Wall, and there they would go to pound out their grief and pour out their hearts.

Jesus continued the pro-tears tradition: "Blessed are those who mourn," he said, "for they will be comforted."

Universal Suffering

When I criss-crossed the United States and Canada offering Isaiah Parish Missions during the past twenty years, I found one thing in common, no matter where I went, no matter the wealth or the poverty of the community, the education or lack of it, people were suffering. They were suffering for many different reasons--death, injury, illness, abuse, bankruptcy, crime, loss of job, etc. etc.

The most common questions I heard, in light of all of these losses, were:

"Why did God make this happen to me?"

"Why did God take my husband/wife/parent from me?"

"Why did God cause the flood/ hurricane/earthquake?"

Usually, these questions were followed by faulty conclusions:

"I was not a good enough person/ husband/wife/parent."

"God is angry with me."

Or, the worst possible conclusion: "It's God's will!"

The first and most important thing that we must realize when we are speaking of suffering and death is that God did not cause any of it. And suffering certainly is not God's will.

Jesus said, "I came so that you may have life, life to the full" (Jn. 10:10). Just as Jesus wept at Lazarus' tomb, he weeps with all of us who are mourning.

Why Do Bad Things Happen to Good People?

I struggled with this question for a long time until a priest friend of mine helped with his explanation. He said that so often people tend to blame God for these horrible events. "In fact," he said, "I don't think God has anything at all to do with these tragedies." He then explained that most tragedies happen for one of three reasons, listed in the sidebar on this page.

Ultimate Healing

And, of course, there is a fourth category called "Mystery." When none of the other three reasons apply, we must simply accept the fact that sometimes we can find no logic, no rhyme nor reason, no rational explanation. Just mystery. This is when we must

Bad things happen because of . . .

1. **Decisions which we ourselves make.** For instance, if we chose to smoke cigarettes and forty years later, we are diagnosed with lung cancer, don't blame it on God. This is a consequence of a decision that we made.

2. **Decisions which other people make, over which we have no control.** If a person decides to drive after drinking , there may be terrible consequences.

3. **The results of natural processes.** For instance the aging process, natural disasters, a genetic proclivity to inherit certain diseases.

"let God be God."

This fourth category, mystery, also includes the fact that, as Christians, we believe that death for believers is the *ultimate* healing. When he or she enters paradise, all tears are wiped from their eyes, and they see God face to face. In this category of mystery, also fall the answers to other common questions which we will never find adequate answers for in this lifetime.

All things Work Together For Good

I find comfort in the words of a retired pastor who told me, "I have suffered many losses during my life -- losing my parents in an automobile accident when I was in seminary, losing a five-year-old nephew to leukemia, and my youngest sister to breast cancer. I used to spend many hours wondering why God would allow these tragedies. I knew that he did not cause them, but why did he permit them to happen? These were all very good people who had long lives ahead of them.

"I finally decided." he continued," that, like it or not, as a man of faith, I must put my trust in God. I *choose* to believe that whatever has happened, whatever will happen, has God's permission and blessing. This is the only way I can make sense of the Scripture verse: 'In all things God works for the good of those who love him' " (Rom. 8:28).

Previous Life-Threatening Incidents

I, too, had pondered these very same questions about God *permitting* the deaths of my children. As I was wrestling with God over this quandary of "Where was God when I needed him?", I remembered a few earlier life-threatening incidents involving my children.

When Danny was three years old, he was run over by a car and, even with tire track marks on his chest, survived without injury! A few years later, when we were at the beach one day, he suddenly was swept out to sea in a riptide and despite my best, terrified efforts, had to be rescued by a life guard.

Years later when Debbie was a junior in high school, she was permitted to drive our old Ford station wagon to high school, chauffering her younger sister Tammy and two other students who also were sisters. One morning they had a terrible accident. A school bus broadsided them and the car was totalled. Miraculously, none of them had a scratch!

And only a few years ago, my son Tommy had all the signs and symptoms of Stage III Hodgkin's disease. After the largest lymph gland was biopsied, I discovered the sweetest six-letter word in our language: *BENIGN!*

Near Misses

Instead of complaining that God could have prevented the deaths of my two children, I began to wonder if God hadn't been true to his promise of sending his angels to keep guard over all of us for many, many years. How many near misses were there that I don't even know about? How many car accidents were prevented by a few seconds' timing? How many illnesses or accidents were nipped in the bud?

Looking back at my own life, what about the time I nearly drowned in a neighbor's pond or the time I fell fifty feet into a well at my uncle's farm? How dare I think that God is not in control? . . .

"Good" . . . At What Price?

While journaling at another time on that scripture passage, "All things work together for good," I thought about the possible "good" that could come from Danny's or Debbie's deaths.

There was the scholarship fund for disadvantaged children that we set up after Danny's death, and now, among other things, there will be a grieving process written after Debbie's death to help others.

But, I then stopped dead in my tracks when I found myself scribbling through my tears these words : "No matter what good comes out of these deaths, the price is too high!"

"The price is too high?" I realized with shock, that the words I just had written might also have been spoken by Mary at the foot of the cross.

Turning Point

Even with my anger, confusion, disappointment, and profound sadness (all of which Mary probably felt also), I had two choices: 1) I could let it all burn and churn within me, futilely searching for answers, or 2) I could try to adjust to their deaths and look forward to seeing them in heaven. The second option offered was Faith; the first, for me, would be Insanity!

It was at that moment that I made a monumental decision, one that I actually made years ago: "I once again *choose* to be a woman of faith, of hope!" (And this conscious recommitment was the turning point for me in my grief the second time around.)

Christian Hope

Hope has always been an absolutely necessary element for growth, stability, healing, recovery, and restoration. Dr. Del Zoppo quotes Elie Wiesel in his book: "It is not given to us to begin; that privilege is God's alone. But it is given to us to *begin again* -- and we do every time we choose to defy death and side with the living. "

The most evocative description of faith in the New Testament is found in Hebrews 11:1, where faith is heralded as "the assurance of things hoped for, the conviction of things not seen."

Jesus said that he came to give us life to the full, abundant life. Life cannot be abundant or to the full if it lacks the element of hope. The joy we know and savor would not be experienced as fully if it were not contrasted with our sadness, tears and doubts.

I have come to a point in my life where I can look back and see that the faith, the experience, and the knowledge that I have gained over a lifetime

> This is my stance today. In spite of my questions and doubts, I *choose* to be a woman of faith, a woman of hope. I *choose* to believe . . . and I *choose* to acknowledge the power and strength of Christ operating within us as we rebuild our lives.

is for a specific purpose, which continues to unfold. This, the Paschal mystery, the cycle of dying and rising in my own life, is coming full circle. Now I am beginning to understand the "whys and wherefores" of the various pathways my life journey has included, all of which underline the power of hope.

"When Bad Things Happen to Good People"

In 1981 Rabbi Harold Kushner wrote a book entitled *When Bad Things Happen to Good People,* as a response to the death of his fourteen-year-old son after suffering from progeria, a fatal disease which promotes rapid aging. This classic in the literature on death and dying has been accepted for decades by people who have been hurt by life. In it he describes many of the ways that people attempt to make sense of their losses when they are grieving. Shown above

---

Reasons People Give For Suffering in Rabbi Kushner's book, all of which he rejects.

1. Suffering comes as a punishment for our sins.

2. Suffering is for some greater, undefined purpose.

 3. Suffering cures us of our faults and makes us better people.

4. Maybe it's a test.

5. It will free us and lead us to a better place.

---

are some of the reasons people give for suffering, which he explores in his book, all of which he rejects.

Rabbi Kushner's Conclusions:

1. "God does not cause our misfortunes. Some are caused by bad luck, some are caused by bad people, and some are simply an inevitable consequence of our being human and being mortal, living in a world of inflexible natural laws."

2. "We will simply have to learn to live with it, sustained and comforted by the knowledge that the earthquake and the accident, the murder and the robbery, are not the will of God, but represent that aspect of reality which stand independent of His will, and which angers and saddens God even as it angers and saddens us."

3. He suggests, "A satisfying response to the tragedies in our lives would be Job's response in Archibald MacLeish's poetic drama, *J. B.* to forgive the world for not being perfect, to forgive God for not making a better world, to reach out to the people around us, and to go on living despite it all."

What does the Church say about Faith and Suffering?

1. Perseverance in Faith: "To live, grow, and persevere in the faith until the end we must nourish it with the word of God; we must beg the Lord to increase our faith (Cf. *Mk* 9:24; *Lk* 17:5; 22:32)" *(CCC #162).*

2. " . . . Even though enlightened by him in whom it believes, faith is often lived in darkness and can be put to the test. The world we live in often seems very far from the one promised us by faith. Our experiences of evil and suffering, injustice, and death, seem to contradict the Good News; they can shake our faith and become a temptation against it" *(CCC 164).*

3. "It is then we must turn to the *witnesses of faith* . . . 'Therefore, since we are surrounded by so great a cloud of witnesses, let us also lay aside every weight, and sin which clings so closely, and let us run with perseverance the race that is set before us, looking to Jesus the pioneer and perfecter of our faith' *(Heb. 12: 1-2)" (CCC #165).*

Reflection/Discussion Questions

1. What were your experiences of the death, funeral home, funeral, burial, reception, if any? Who was there? What do you remember most?

_____
_____
_____
_____
_____
_____
_____

2. How are you dealing with understanding your loved one's death?

_____
_____
_____
_____
_____
_____
_____

3. Can you remember times in the past when you felt God intervened in protecting or saving a loved one's life?

_____
_____
_____
_____
_____

4. Does your loved one's death fall into one of the first three causes of why bad things happen to good people? Or, the fourth? Explain.

_____
_____
_____
_____
_____
_____

Ponderings . . .

What does the Church say?

Hope is defined as "the theological virtue by which we desire the kingdom of heaven and eternal life as our happiness, placing our trust in Christ's promises and relying not on our own strength, but on the help of the grace of the Holy Spirit" (CCC #1817).

"The virtue of hope responds to the aspiration to happiness which God has placed in the heart of every man; it takes up the hopes that inspire men's activities and purifies them so as to order them to the Kingdom of heaven; it keeps man from discouragement; it sustains him during times of abandonment; it opens up his heart in expectation of eternal beatitude" (CCC #1818).

Scripture:

2 Corinthians 12:8-9 -- "Three times I pleaded with the Lord to take it (the thorn in my flesh) away from me. But he said to me, 'My grace is sufficent for you, for my power is made perfect in weakness.'"

Colossians 1:24 -- "Even now I find my joy in the suffering I endure for you. In my own flesh I fill up what is lacking in the sufferings of Christ for the sake of his body, the church."

Food for Thought:

"God does not want us to live in darkness. In the 23rd Psalm, we read, 'I walk through the valley of death . . .'; it does not say that we stay there!" . . . *Valli Leone, an Isaiah lay presenter.*

"All shall be well, and all shall be well, and all manner of thing shall be well." *Julian of Norwich*

Practical Suggestions:

1. Set aside your search for answers for awhile. They can be searing and burning up your energy, all of which you need now.

2. If you cannot set these aside now and have questions concerning the meaning of your loved one's death which are sapping you of energy or distracting you from your "grief-work," make an appointment with a priest or spiritual director.

3. If you are having a faith crisis, many grief therapists suggest that you set aside, for the moment, any questions concerning your faith until you have worked through some of your other grief issues.

Prayerful Suggestions:
1. Write down five more things that you are grateful for on your gratitude list.
2. Pray the Sorrowful Mysteries.
3. Meditate on the lyrics of the hymn, "Future Full of Hope."
4. Thank God for the unknown protection you have received.

Homework for Session IV:
Please review the "Reactions to Trauma" list in the next session and rate them, according to the instructions there.

Closing Prayer
God of the Grieving, God of the Mourners, we know that you weep with us and for us. Extend your gentle hand and wipe away our tears as we suffer the deepest pain we have even known. We thank you and praise you for being with our loved ones when they were suffering. Be with us as we continue on our journey of sadness and healing. In Jesus's name, we pray, Amen.

"I Did Not Die"
Do not stand at my grave and weep.
I am not there, I do not sleep.
I am a thousand winds that blow;
I am the diamond glints on fallen snow.
I am the sunlight on the ripened grain.
I am the gentle autumn rain.

When you awaken I am the morning hush,
I am the swift uplifting rush
Of quiet birds in circle flight.
I am the stars that shine at night.

Do not stand at my grave and cry.
I am not there. I did not die.

Journaling

Date: _____

1. A significant event that occurred this week.
2. The person who was most important to me this week.
3. Changes I observe happening to me.
4. My plans for next week include . . .
5. Notes to myself . . .

_____
_____
_____
_____
_____
_____
_____
_____
_____
_____
_____
_____
_____
_____
_____
_____
_____
_____
_____
_____
_____
_____
_____

Session Four
BROKENNESS

"The world breaks everyone, and afterward
many are strong at the broken places."
Ernest Hemingway

Prayer: + In the name of the Father and of the Son and of the Holy Spirit, Amen. God our Father, we are so broken and falling apart in so many ways as we grieve our loved ones. We honor and praise your goodness, and we thank you for your assurance that you are with us through it all. Pour out your Spirit upon us and strengthen our desire to be your faithful people. Heal us in all our broken places and give us your peace and new life during this time. We ask this in Jesus' name. Amen.

Scripture: II Corinthians 4: 8-9 "We are afflicted in every way possible, but we are not crushed; full of doubts, we never despair. We are persecuted but never abandoned; we are struck down but never destroyed."

Hymn Meditation: **"Taste and See"**

Refrain: **Taste and see the goodness of the Lord, the goodness of the Lord.**

**I will bless the Lord at all times. His praise is always on my lips.
In the Lord my soul shall sing. The humble shall hear me and be glad.**

**Glorify the Lord with me. Together let us praise his name.
I called the Lord and he answered me. From all my fears he set me free.**

**The angel of the Lord watches you. He cares for all who love the Lord.
Taste and see how good is God. How happy are they who seek his love.**

STRESS, CRISIS, TRAUMA

Ground Zero

Often, our reactions to traumatic events are similar to the ways that we react to the death of our loved ones. For instance, what was your first reaction to hearing or seeing on television the actual events of the terrorist attacks on September 11th? If you were like most people, you were numb with disbelief. "Oh my God, this can't be happening!" "This isn't real!" you cried! This is similar to the first stage of grief -- shock and denial.

These statements, along with the feelings of being numb with disbelief, are classic examples of shock. For instance, when the events of September 11th occurred, I was numb, shocked. That afternoon, as I continued watching television accounts of the tragedy, I became so cold that I had to take a hot shower, put on flannel pajamas (the warmest thing I own, living in South Florida), a quilted robe (the next warmest thing), and cover myself with a blanket. And I was still shivering for hours afterward, well into the evening. Later, my doctor said it was a classic case of shock.

All we could see were the ruins and the rubble of Ground Zero, the remains of the trauma, and at this early stage of grief after losing a loved one .....that's all we can see.....the ruins and the rubble, symbolized by our plant now. This may be a stark image for you to consider, but it symbolizes the reality and finality of death.

Even if the death of your loved one was expected after a long illness or if your loved one was quite elderly and had lived a long life, there is still a sense of shock. Death is so final!

Stress, Crisis, Trauma

On a scale of "stress, crisis, trauma" (as in the Holmes-Rahe Social Readjustment Rating Scale,) the death of a spouse is the number one highest cause of stress. The death of a "close family

> **Thinking that you are going crazy is NORMAL!!!!!**

member" ranks fifth after divorce, marital separation and a jail term. I would argue that placement, but . . . the point is that the deaths of loved ones are considered trauma instead of mere crisis or stress.

When death comes to a loved one, our lives change forever. After an initial period of shock and disbelief, we enter into a phase of mourning which seems like it will last forever. We experience many different symptoms, some of them quite severely.

Not only do we ache all over with physical responses to this "protest" to our loss, but we are convinced we are surely losing our mind.

We are often confused or disoriented; we forget everything. Insanity becomes more and more of a possibility, we think to ourselves. We cannot remember anything; we cannot concentrate longer than a few minutes.

A flood of various feelings and thoughts rage within us, and we may have some serious issues with our faith. The most important thing to remember about any of these symptoms is that they are normal and eventually will go away.

Please rate yourself on the "Reactions to Trauma" list of symptoms found below so that you will be able to refer to it in six months and a year from now to see how you are progressing in your recovery from your loss.

However, if any symptoms persist intensely, be sure to consult your personal physician.

REACTIONS TO GRIEF

If you have experienced any of these symptoms, please rate the degree of severity at the present time (in the past two weeks.) Save this workbook and rate these symptoms again after six months and a year from now.

Scale:	1 = Slight	2 = Moderate	3 = Intense
	(Date: ____)	(Date: ____)	(Date: ____)
Symptom	Now	6 Months	1 Year

Physical Reactions to Grief:

		Now	6 Months	1 Year
1.	Fatigue/exhaustion	____	____	____
2.	Sleep disturbance	____	____	____
3.	Underactivity/overactivity	____	____	____
4.	Change in appetite	____	____	____
5.	Digestive problems	____	____	____
6.	Nightmares	____	____	____
7.	Muscle tremors/twitches	____	____	____

8.	Startle reactions	_____	_____	_____
9.	Headaches	_____	_____	_____
10.	Dizziness	_____	_____	_____
11.	Muscle aches	_____	_____	_____
12.	Vomiting	_____	_____	_____
13.	Rapid heartbeat	_____	_____	_____
14.	Deep Sighing	_____	_____	_____
15.	Tearfulness	_____	_____	_____
16.	Weight gain/loss	_____	_____	_____
17.	Headaches.	_____	_____	_____
18.	High blood pressure	_____	_____	_____
19.	Lowered immunity	_____	_____	_____
20.	Shaky voice	_____	_____	_____
21.	Other	_____	_____	_____
22.	Other	_____	_____	_____

Cognitive Reactions:

1.	Difficulty concentrating	_____	_____	_____
2.	Difficulty solving problems	_____	_____	_____
3.	Flashbacks of the loss	_____	_____	_____
4.	Difficulty in making decisions	_____	_____	_____
5.	Memory disturbance	_____	_____	_____
6.	Worrying	_____	_____	_____
7.	Isolation/withdrawal	_____	_____	_____
8.	Preoccupation with the loss	_____	_____	_____
9.	Lowered attention span	_____	_____	_____
10.	Slower thinking	_____	_____	_____
11.	Naming familiar objects/people	_____	_____	_____
12.	Language errors	_____	_____	_____
13.	Forgetfulness	_____	_____	_____
14.	Loss of creativity, productivity	_____	_____	_____
15.	Mental blocks	_____	_____	_____
16.	Preoccupation with past	_____	_____	_____
17.	Thoughts of death or suicide	_____	_____	_____
18.	Other	_____	_____	_____
19.	Other	_____	_____	_____
20.	Other	_____	_____	_____

Scale:	1 = Slight	2 = Moderate	3 = Intense

Symptom	Now	6 Months	1 Year
Emotional Reactions:			
1. Guilt	____	____	____
2. Feelings of helplessness	____	____	____
3. Emotional numbing	____	____	____
4. Overly sensitive	____	____	____
5. Dread	____	____	____
6. Sadness	____	____	____
7. Amnesia for the event	____	____	____
8. Fear/anxiety	____	____	____
9. Irritability	____	____	____
10. Withdrawal/isolation	____	____	____
11. Self-doubt	____	____	____
12. Moodiness	____	____	____
13. Hypervigilance	____	____	____
14. Moodiness	____	____	____
15. Loneliness	____	____	____
16. Shame	____	____	____
17. Anger which may be manifested by:			
a. Scapegoating	____	____	____
b. Irritability	____	____	____
c. Frustration with bureaucracy	____	____	____
d. Violent fantasies	____	____	____
18. Other	____	____	____
19. Other	____	____	____

Spiritual Reactions to Grief:

	Now	6 Months	1 Year
1. Anger with God	____	____	____
2. Guilt	____	____	____
3. Unforgiveness	____	____	____
4. Inability to pray	____	____	____
5. Search for meaning	____	____	____
6. Questions for God	____	____	____
7. Unable to attend church	____	____	____
8. Questioning of faith	____	____	____

Scale:	1 = Slight	2 = Moderate	3 = Intense

Symptom	Now	6 Months	1 Year
9. Angry with church	____	____	____
10. Angry with priests	____	____	____
11. Decreased spirituality	____	____	____
12. Abandonment by God	____	____	____
13. Abandonment by clergy	____	____	____
13. Distrust of tenets of faith	____	____	____
14. Uncertainty of everlasting life	____	____	____
15. Other	____	____	____

Depression:
People sometimes experience a period of mild to moderate depression following exposure to a stressful event or tragic loss.

Loss/gain in weight
Insomnia
Lethargy/low energy
Social withdrawal
Difficulty concentrating

Persistent sad mood
Isolation
Intrusive thoughts
(See your doctor if any of these symptoms last for several weeks.)

Healing -- A Choice
Adjustment -- A Choice

For those of us who are grieving, there are now irreversible losses which no amount of faith can reverse in this world. The world as we knew it simply no longer exists. We cannot return to yesterday or yesteryear.

In order for emotional and spiritual healing to occur, we must acknowledge the reality of our loss. This is what the grieving process is all about. It is not until we can acknowledge the reality and face the finality of our losses that we can choose to move on to acceptance or, as I

God tells us in Scripture: "See, I set before you today life and propserity, death and destruction. . . . This day I call heaven and earth as witnesses against you, that I have set before you life and death, blessings and curses. Now choose life, so that you and your children may live and that you may love the LORD your God, listen to his voice, and hold fast to him. For the Lord is your life . . ." (Deut. 30:15, 19-20)

prefer to call it, adjustment. Adjustment is a choice. We can choose to recover and regain our strength after traumatic life events. Or we can choose to remain in the ashes, licking our wounds.

Time alone does not heal, if we choose to keep the wound open and festering. We could choose to focus on death. God urges us to focus on life.

We have the assurance that God journeys with us in our pain and in our sadness. Our faith allows us to survive, to live *through*, to live *with* the pain, the mystery, the loss and come out on the other side--Resurrection! Life has not ended; it has changed.

Acceptance/adjustment is necessary for our spiritual and emotional healing, as an individual. But acceptance is not mere resignation. Acceptance is openly acknowledging the facts that because of my loss (and secondary losses resulting from the primary loss,) my world is no longer the same. With this knowledge and acceptance, we can move on. We can make adjustments to accommodate a new and changing world for ourselves.

Perhaps herein lies the wisdom of the Serenity Prayer -- in knowing what changes we can make, what changes we cannot make, and having the wisdom to know the difference. Life will not be the same, but it will be life. It will be different. But with a God of love and mercy beside us, it can be life to the full.

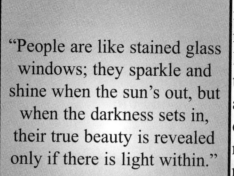

"People are like stained glass windows; they sparkle and shine when the sun's out, but when the darkness sets in, their true beauty is revealed only if there is light within."

Dr. Elizabeth Kubler Ross

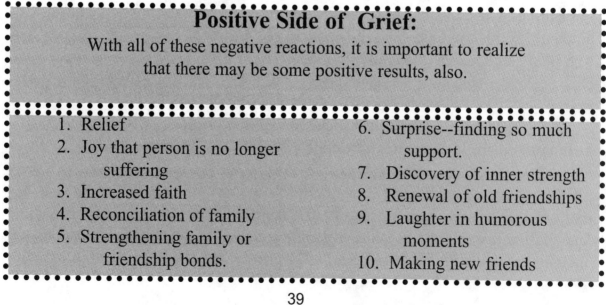

Positive Side of Grief:

With all of these negative reactions, it is important to realize that there may be some positive results, also.

1. Relief
2. Joy that person is no longer suffering
3. Increased faith
4. Reconciliation of family
5. Strengthening family or friendship bonds.
6. Surprise--finding so much support.
7. Discovery of inner strength
8. Renewal of old friendships
9. Laughter in humorous moments
10. Making new friends

Reflection/Discussion Questions

1. Where were you on September 11th? What were your reactions then? Were there any similarities to your reactions to the loss of your loved one?

_____

_____

_____

_____

_____

2. Can you remember another time in your life when you experienced any of these symptoms? How did you handle these symptoms then? What worked and what didn't?

_____

_____

_____

_____

3. Is there any one symptom which is bothering you more than others?

_____

_____

_____

_____

4. Have you expressed your thoughts or feelings about God? How? If not, what do you plan to do about them? When?

_____

_____

_____

5. Do you feel that there is any part of you that simply does not want to get on with the process of adjusting and healing? If so, can you tell us about it?

_____

_____

_____

_____

Healing Service

Participant #1: +Gracious God, Creator of All the World, we thank you and praise you for being present to us at this time of sorrow. Thank you for walking with us in our pain, in our loss, in all of the symptoms of grief that we may be experiencing. We ask your healing hands to touch us now as we prepare to go forth for another week. Send your angels to guide and protect us. Help us to taste and see your goodness, O Lord. We ask in the name of Jesus, Amen.

Participant #2: A reading from St. Paul to the Corinthians. "We are afflicted in every way possible, but we are not crushed; full of doubts, we never despair. We are persecuted but never abandoned; we are struck down but never destroyed" (*II Corinthians 4: 8-9*).

Litany

Leader: Ask each participant to name one symptom they are suffering with (e.g."For depression, For confusion. For insomnia". . . whatever . . . and then the group responds "Lord, come to our assistance." Then the next participant . . until all have had a chance to name symptom or problems or challenges they are experiencing.) Let us now listen to our meditative hymn:

"Taste and See"

Refrain: **Taste and see the goodness of the Lord, the goodness of the Lord.**

**I will bless the Lord at all times. His praise is always on my lips.
In the Lord my soul shall sing. The humble shall hear me and be glad.**

**Glorify the Lord with me. Together let us praise his name.
I called the Lord and he answered me. From all my fears he set me free.**

The angel of the Lord watches you. He cares for all who love the Lord.

Taste and see how good is God. How happy are they who seek his love.

Closing Prayer: Loving God, we know that your love for us is beyond undstanding and that when we weep, you weep. Comfort us as we taste the bitter wine of grief and the salty tears of death. Help us to acknowledge and ease the suffering and pain of your broken and suffering Body. We ask this in the name of your son, Jesus Christ, who lives and reigns with you forever and ever. Amen.

Ponderings . . .

What does the Church say about illness, suffering?

"Illness and suffering have always been among the gravest problems confronted in human life. In illness, man experiences his powerlessness, his limitations, and his finitude. Every illness can make us glimpse death . . .

". . . By his passion and death on the cross Christ has given a new meaning to suffering: it can henceforth configure us to him and unite us with his redemptive Passion" (CCC #1500, 1505).

Scripture:

"Comfort, comfort my people,
says your God."
Is.40: 1.

Practical Suggestions:

1. If you have not yet done so, rate your symptoms on the list in this chapter.
2. Give yourself permission to vent your feelings about these symptoms in healthy ways such as prayer, writing, talking, exercise, meditation.
3. Write down the specifics of what you are seeking from the Lord at this time in your life. Define the healing that you are seeking.
4. Recall times when sacraments, prayer, or scripture played a big part in healing in your life or others.
5. Add five more items to your "Gratitude List." (Have you gotten to "beautiful sunrises" or "chocolate ice cream" yet?)

Prayerful Suggestions:

1. Ask God to help you come to accept the areas in your life that need healing. Pray to God, asking for your healing.
2. Read Psalm 121 and memorize the last line: "The Lord will watch over your coming and going, both now and forevermore." Repeat this whenever you are feeling fearful or anxious.
3. If your symptoms are quite serious, ask for the Anointing of the Sick.

Homework: None. Relax. Take good care of yourself.

Journaling

Date: _____

1. A significant event that occurred this week.
2. The person who was most important to me this week.
3. Changes I observe happening to me.
4. My plans for next week include . . .
5. Notes to myself . . .

_____

_____

_____

_____

_____

_____

_____

_____

_____

_____

_____

_____

_____

_____

_____

_____

_____

_____

_____

_____

_____

_____

_____

_____

Session Five

STUMBLING BLOCKS

Opening Prayer: + In the name of the Father and of the Son and of the Holy Spirit. Amen.   Gracious God, we ask you to transform our pain, our losses, and our confusion into wisdom and acceptance. We ask you to help us overcome any stumbling blocks that obstruct or prolong the grieving process. We ask you to help us to deal with our unforgiveness of others and to seek and accept our own forgiveness. We ask this through Jesus, who in his life showed mercy and forgiveness to all. Amen.

Scripture: "The father said to his servants . . . 'Let us celebrate because this son of mine was dead and has come back to life. He was lost and is found.' "
(Luke 15: 22,24)

Meditation Hymn:

"Prodigal Son"

Refrain -- **My heart was full of joy as I saw you on the road.**
With outstretched arms I ran to hold you again.
My love for you will always be strong.
Welcome home, my prodigal son, Welcome home, my son.

You've been gone for a long time and you've traveled many roads.
You've struggled and suffered, felt hunger and pain.
But now that you're home and with me again,
I give you a banquet and welcome you in.

Your heart became restless. You felt that you must go.
I gave you your share, and on down the road you went.
My heart was heavy, a tear I did shed,
but I knew that someday you'd come home again.

Stumbling Blocks

What are some of the stumbling blocks we might face in coping with our grief? What may be prohibiting or prolonging the process of healing? Denial? Unforgiveness? Anger? Anxiety? Powerlessness? Regrets? Resentment? The sense that our faith is not strong enough?

Unforgiveness

Of all the behaviors named above, unforgiveness is one of the most serious spiritual stumbling blocks to the healing process. Sometimes hurtful events may occur surrounding the death involving our loved one. Family members or friends may need to be forgiven. Or, we ourselves, may need to be for-given. It is sometimes difficult to admit the need for forgiveness, for that affirms our humanity, the fact that we are not perfect, and we do make mistakes.

We might have many regrets about things we said, or didn't say, things other people or our loved one said or didn't say, did or didn't do . . . and so on. How many of us wouldn't like to live over the last days or months prior to our loved one's death?

Regrets and Resentment

Perhaps we carry guilt along with our regrets surrounding our loved one's death: "I am so sorry that we had this huge argument the night before he died," or, "I really hurt my mother-in-law the last time I spoke with her. I am so sorry."

Sometimes, the guilt is what we call inappropriate guilt, for instance when people say, "I am so sorry that I was not at my loved one's bedside when he died." (This, in spite of the fact that the person had spent many days and nights at the hospice or hospital and had just gone home to get some rest. Guilt is inappropriate here.)

Some examples of resentment are: "I will never forgive that doctor under any under circumstances!" or "After what she said at the funeral, she is the last person on this earth that I would ever consider forgiving!"

Forgiving: For Your Own Sake

Our inability to forgive takes its toll on us physically, emotionally and spiritually. Not forgiving someone takes a lot of energy! And, as we all know, we are the ones hurt by our hatred or anger. In many cases, the person we need to forgive is not even aware of our unforgiveness or for the need for forgiveness in the first place!

When we forgive someone from the heart, we are doing ourselves a great favor! Harbored resentments, anger, hurt feelings -- even when they are justified -- simply poison our own system. Festering under the surface, these hurts become more and more painful. Eventually they come to a head and either burst or their poison spreads to other parts of our lives or bodies. Physicians will tell us that pent-up anger often leads to stroke, heart disease, depression and self-anguish.

The trick is to forgive from the heart, not from the head, since the latter only leads to the same resentments and anger continuing to resurface. We think we have forgiven someone and find that, in the long run, we resent them even more.

But, when we simply *cannot* forgive someone in our heart, then we turn to God and ask God to forgive that person for us, since we truly are unable to do so at this time. "Father in Heaven, forgive the nurses who were so careless." "Father, forgive John for his angry words when his brother was so sick." Our God is a merciful God.

"Forgiving the Unforgivable"

A few years ago one of the popular women's magazines ran a story about a woman whose granddaughter was kidnapped, horribly abused, raped, murdered, and left in a garbage bin behind a restaurant. I cannot remember the exact details in the article, but the title of the article was, "Forgiving the Unforgivable." The child's murderer was found, convicted, and sentenced to death.

For the longest time, the grandmother could not even go near the restaurant where they found the child. But one day, she went to visit her pastor and told him of her horrible suffering and especially her inability to forgive the murderer. After weeks and weeks of counseling and prayer, she finally was able to forgive the man, and she found a remarkable sense of freedom and peace. She was no longer using an enormous amount of negative energy to hate this man.

Much to her surprise, she soon found herself regretting that he had been sentenced to death. She thought to herself, "Violence only begets more violence. We are doing the very thing to him that he did to my beloved grandchild!" She began to protest the death penalty for this man, but eventually he was executed.

She has gone on, though, to found a ministry which opposes the death penalty in her state. This is definitely a story of a woman who was able to "forgive the unforgivable!"

Forgiveness is a Gift

At many times in my own life, I have found that forgiveness, the ability to forgive, has been a gift handed to me on a silver platter. In Danny's case, it has saved me light-years of anger and wasted energy. I think of the Scripture verse, "Every good and perfect gift is from above, coming down from the Father of the heavenly lights" (James 1:17). All good gifts come from God. Forgiveness certainly qualifies as a good gift. Ask for it!

Forgiveness -- An Act of the Will

Forgiveness is an act of the will. Often forgiveness does not result in an immediate change in our feelings. However, repeated decisions to choose to forgive often result in a gradual change in our

---

What forgiveness is and is not:

Forgiveness is an act of our free will.

We do not have to feel forgiving to forgive.

Forgiveness means I let go of the desire for revenge.

Forgiveness seeks restoration of the relationship, even in death.

Forgiveness frees me to get on with my life.

Forgiveness does not ignore the hurt, or ignore painful unmet needs, or gloss over anger.

Forgiveness does not mean 'forgive and forget.'

Forgiveness does not erase the memory of the hurt, but it gradually drains the memory of the pain surrounding the hurt.

Without forgiveness, healing will not occur.

---

feelings toward that person. The quality of our forgiveness is not measured by our feelings, but by the firmness of our decision to forgive.

The Sweetness of Reconciliation

Forgiveness just involves one person; reconciliation involves two or more people. When we truly repent and say we are sorry to God, there is no such thing as God dismissing or ignoring our apology. There is no such thing as long-term resentment or anger on God's part. God always forgives.

Why?Because God loves us unconditionally. When we say we are sorry for offending God or others, including ourselves, God does not reject us. God forgives us and rejoices with us.

This unconditional love is the beauty and sweetness surrounding the story of the Prodigal Son. The father loves the wayward son unconditionally, . . . and the fatted calf is slain for a feast. "My son was lost, but now is found."

Reconciliation with God is a two-way street. The good news is that if you move even an inch toward reconciliation, God will meet you more than half-way and encourage you to come the rest of the way. And then the Father will dance!

"Forgiveness Service"

At the end of this session, we will have a "Forgiveness Service." This would be a good time for you to ask forgiveness for those words or actions which you regret or to ask for forgiveness for the people who have caused resentments in your life. Often we can forgive everyone else, but not ourselves, so be sure to ask for forgiveness for yourself, too.

This "Forgiveness Service" is not the Sacrament of Reconciliation, and if you are dealing with serious sin, you need to go to Confession which is offered regularly in your parish.

Psalm 23
A Contemporary Paraphrase

God is my friend. What more could I want?
God sits with me in the quiet times of my life,
God explores with me the meaning of my life.
God calls me forth as a whole person.

Even though I walk along paths of pain, prejudice, hatred and
depression, my fears are quieted because God is with me.
God's words and thoughts challenge me.
God causes me to be sensitive to the needs of mankind,
then lifts up opportunities for serving.
God's confidence stretches me.
Surely love shall be mine to share throughout my life,
and I shall be sustained by God's concern forever.
(Author Unknown)

Reflection/Discussion Questions

*(**Note:** The facilitator will provide paper hearts for you to jot down regrets, resentments or people you need to forgive. These will be used during the Forgiveness Service, at the end of this session.)*

1. Were there any incidents during your loved one's illness, death, or funeral that you now regret happening?

_____

_____

_____

_____

2. Are there people in your life whom you need to forgive? Or are there people in your life who need to forgive you?

_____

_____

_____

_____

3. If you could go back to the time the illness began or when you first heard of the unexpected death, would you like anything to have been done differently?

_____

_____

_____

_____

4. If your loved one were still alive, what would you say? (Write a letter to your loved one . . . see pages at end of this session.)

_____

_____

_____

_____

5. Is there one thing more than any other that you regret and wish you could do over? How would you do it differently?

_____

_____

_____

_____

Forgiveness Service

Presenter: We are all in a process, leading to deeper degrees of forgiveness and healing. But no matter where we are in the process of grieving, one thing is certain: God loves us. No matter how we feel, no matter what has happened to us, no matter how lonely we are, no matter how deeply we mourn, we belong to God, nestled in his heart. Therefore, as children of God, we freely ask for forgiveness for ourselves and for others.

In Scripture we read: "The father said to his servants . . . 'Let us have a feast and celebrate. For this son of mine was dead and is alive again; he was lost and now is found.' "   *Luke 15: 22,24)*

Let us ask ourselves these questions *(and jot down the answers on the paper hearts, if this has not already been done. Read slowly, allowing time for thought.)*
>   Are there people in circumstances surrounding the death of
>   your loved one that you need to forgive?

>   . . . doctors, nurses, other professional people? . . . family members,
>   friends? . . . God? . . yourself?. . .

>   Are there any of your own words or actions that you regret?

>   Are there any words or actions of others that you resent?

(Ritual action): When you are finished writing your regrets or resentments, please tear the paper hearts into tiny pieces and put them into the pitcher of tears. *(You may want to play "The Prodigal Son" again . . or the first song on the CD, "Love Never Fails" as background music.)* We are in the process of dissolving our regrets and resentments in our tears of forgiveness. Now, I will anoint each of you with our tears as a sign of God's forgiveness for us and our forgiveness for others. (Dip your thumb into the pitcher and then make the sign of the cross on each person's forehead, saying "I bless you in the name of the Father, and of the Son, and of the Holy Spirit. Amen.)

All: Our Father….
P: May the peace and love and compassion of our lord Jesus Christ be with us all now and forever. Amen.

Ponderings . . .

What does the Church say?

"Nothing causes us to so nearly resemble God as the forgiveness of injuries." *St. John of Chrysostom*

Supportive Scripture: "If we say we have no sin, we deceive ourselves and the truth is not in us. If we confess our sins, he is faithful and just, and will forgive our sins and cleanse us from all unrighteousness." *I John 1: 8 - 9*

Practical Suggestions:

1. If you are truly concerned that you need to apologize to someone or ask forgiveness, write a thoughtful letter to that person.
2. Be kind to yourself at this time. Do not be too hard on yourself. You may be operating out of an exaggerated sensitivity.

Prayerful Suggestions:

1. God has forgiven you. In what ways have you not forgiven yourself?
2. Stop beating yourself up. If negative thoughts or feelings of in appropriate guilt beckon, just "don't go there."

Food for Thought:

"God created us *without* us: but he did not will to save us *without* us."

St. Augustine

"To err is human, to forgive divine." *Alexander Pope*

"For the religious person to do wrong is to defy his King; for the Christian, it is to wound his Friend." *William Temple*

"The greatest fault is to be conscious of none." *Thomas Carlyle*

"I see no fault that I might not have committed myself." *Goethe*

Homework:

1. Add five more items to your Gratitude List. (Favorite vacation memories, your grandmother, dishwashers, computers?)
2. Consider writing a letter to your loved one. (See end of session.)

51

Journaling

Date: _____

1. A significant event that occurred this week.
2. The person who was most important to me this week.
3. Changes I observe happening to me.
4. My plans for next week include . . .
5. Notes to myself . . .

_____

_____

_____

_____

_____

_____

_____

_____

_____

_____

_____

_____

_____

_____

_____

_____

_____

_____

_____

_____

_____

_____

_____

_____

_____

_____

_____

Letter to My Loved One

Date _____

Dear _____.

     I haven't written to you lately, but there are a few things on my mind that I would like to share with you. First of all . . .

                         Love,

PS --I forgot to tell you . . .

Letter From My Loved One

Date _____

Dear _____,

    I haven't written to you lately, either, and there are a few things on my mind, too, that I would like to share with you. First of all . . .

Love,

PS --I forgot to tell you . . .

Session Six
FAMILY, COMMUNITY

Opening Prayer:

+In the name of the Father and of the Son and of the Holy Spirit. God of Life,we thank you for all the assistance and strength you have given us so far. Yet, there are days when the new burdens we carry are so heavy that we need help from you and our friends and family. You have promised that you will always be with us, and we trust that you will be at our side now during this time of sorrow and loss. We ask this confidently in the name of your beloved son, Jesus Christ, who lives and reigns now and forever, amen.

Scripture: "Fear not, for I have redeemed you;
I have called you by name: you are mine."
Isaiah 43:1

Meditation Hymn:
"Because I Love You"
(For the parish community of St. Joseph, Crescent Springs, Kentucky)

Refrain -- **I have called you by name; you are mine, says the Lord.
You are precious to me, be not afraid, because I love you.**

**If you pass through raging waters, you shall not drown.
If you walk through roaring fire, you shall not be burned.**

**Do not fear for I am with you until the end of time.
I call you sons and daughters, forever you are mine.**

**Let my people come together. Proclaim the news.
The blind shall see and the deaf shall hear.**

**I have called you one and all to witness to my word.
I am your Lord, the God of Israel.**

Symbol: The empty container reminds us of the empty tomb. Christ did what he promised; he overcame death for us. The empty container also reminds us once again that our loved ones are no longer present to us physically. The empty tomb also may represent a feeling of "emptiness" or loss.

We must remember, though that we are not alone. Our friends, family, and the community of saints surrounds and supports us.

The Good News is that without the empty tomb, there is no resurrection. Without accepting the fact that our loved one's life has changed but not ended, there is no healing or adjustment to the reality of our loss.

It was only with the Good News that Christ had risen from the dead that the apostles and disciples were able to begin to live again! And the same goes for us!

Secondary Losses

While we are all very aware of our primary loss, the loss of our loved ones, we may not realize that we also have secondary losses. Sometimes we can name them, but sometimes they are somewhat elusive. The more obvious ones are relational in nature. These are losses such as actively being someone's wife or mother, or husband or father, or brother or sister, or friend.

If the son you lost was a star baseball player on the Little League team, you have lost that status. If your father had been the President of the Bank, you no longer have certain social privileges which he shared with the family. (You will *always* be the father of a star baseball player or the bank president's daughter, but you have lost the *present* relationship with that person through death.)

So, as we see, there are many different types of "relational secondary losses," but there are also other types of secondary losses.

Social losses include not being a couple anymore and all the social implications that go with it, your desire not to be with people socially, your desire to stay at home alone.

Intellectual losses include loss of clear thinking, loss of memory, loss of concentration, loss of interest.

Physical losses may include loss of energy, sleep, appetite, exercise, health and others.

Spiritual loss may include loss of faith, loss of trust in God, loss of security of church membership, loss of ability to pray.

Emotional losses may include loss of a sense of emotional stability, loss of ability to love deeply again, loss of sense of peace, well-being, joy. A common feeling is that you will never laugh again.

So, while you are still experiencing the pain of the primary loss, it is compounded by a variety of secondary losses which also must be "worked through" in the grieving process.

People Who Need People

Independence has been defined as someone saying, "I don't need anyone: I can stand alone on my own two feet."

Dependence is defined as someone saying, "I can't stand alone at all; I must constantly lean on you!"

Interdependence is when people say, "I need you and you need me; let's lean on each other!"

As you are learning to live without your loved one, you may be experiencing all three: independence, dependence and interdependence.

Of course, we all know that no one can stand alone . . . at least, not for very long. Independence is sometimes seen as a mask being worn as a defense mechanism or protective shield.

And the opposite, dependence, is quite acceptable . . . if you are a child. Some people who are grieving become so totally dependent on other people that they begin to lose their own life, their own spirit. Some of this is known as "learned helplessness" when others insist on doing *everything* for the one who is grieving. In some cases, soon the griever realizes how easy life has become and chooses to be dependent for the rest of his/her life. This is not healthy. A little bit of dependence is good for the soul, but not unnecessary,

life-long dependency. A person can actually regress in skills and health, if he/she is not challenged to take on some responsibility.

Now obviously, I am not speaking of people who are incapacitated physically, mentally, or emotionally. But I will add one caution concerning the use of prescription drugs. If one becomes dependent on sleeping pills or anti-depression medication, many side effects can mimic a mild incapacitation (such as memory loss, confusion, etc.)

Interdependence in relationships is the healthy medium between the other two at normal times of our lives. Interdependence could be one of the most important goals of your period of grieving. It is difficult, though, because grieving is so self-centered.

All About You

The grief process, by definition, is all about you! It is about how *you* are going to work through *your* grief. As the old gospel hymn says, "You've gotta walk this lonesome valley; you've gotta walk it by yourself; nobody else will walk it for you. You gotta walk it by yourself!"

No matter how many books you read, or how many support groups you attend, or how much professional counseling you receive, no one except you can work through your grief. Someone once asked me "If I go to this support group, will it cure my grief?" The answer is "No, it would give you some direction along the bumpy road ahead, but you would only get out of it what you put into it. There is no 'cure' for grief."

One of the turning points in my own grief, indicating that I was moving ahead from the intense acute grieving stage, was that I began looking outside of my own self-centeredness. This is not pejorative at all, simply a fact that we are so totally consumed by the pain of grief that we often cannot see others around us.

Do Unto Others . . .

You are most fortunate if you have family and friends around you who will see you through your grief in the long run. One of the ways this happens, especially with other family members is that you need to see them through *their* grief for the long run.

Instead of applying superficial bandaids to the emotional wounds of my other children and grandchildren, or to my husband, who also was grieving the loss of stepchildren, I now found myself being much more concerned about how *they* were doing than before. Their cares and concerns became my cares and concerns, and vice versa. I had to remember that they were also grieving the loss of a sister or brother or aunt or stepchild.

Widows, particularly, have told me that their "loss of tunnel vision" was a turning point for them as they realized how much their children were hurting, too. This is not to say that we were insensitive to the needs of others in the early stage of grief, but that while we cared greatly about them, we hurt so badly that there was little we could do for them.

Ask for Help

When we lose family members, we also lose certain functions that they fulfilled for us. Not just "jobs" such as paying bills, taking care of the car, raking the leaves. But of functions such as being someone to talk to, or someone who took us to the grocery store, or someone we could often visit and enjoy.

Now we must be able (sometimes despite others' expectations that we must be independent) to ask for help freely. Family and friends will be happy to help us at this time. People often ask, "What can we do for you?" Well, tell them!

But, also, when you are able, remember to ask them what you can do for them.

Community Support

Outside of your small community of family and friends, there are larger communities that also will offer you support -- your local community and your faith community.

If you feel that you are not progressing through the grief process, do not hesitate to consult a counselor for an evaluation to see if he/she thinks that you would benefit by counseling sessions. There are counselors who specialize in grief management. Also, most local hospices offer free counseling by their staff social workers. "Camp Good Grief" is a weekend away for children who have suffered the loss of loved ones, also provided free of charge by participating hospices.

Specialized support groups are also available, ranging from Alzheimer's victims' families to military widows to parents of murdered children. Also, clergy and trained pastoral counselors are available through the Church, as are spiritual directors.

The Role of Sacraments

We have many resources in our faith community to help us through the healing process: sacraments, scripture, prayer, the community of believers.

The Sacrament of Reconciliation is extremely beneficial in the healing of anger, resentment, and sinfulness. Without forgiveness, healing and salvation can not occur. (The Latin root word of salvation is *salve*, as in salve that we put on a wound and is used in the process of healing.)

The Sacrament of Eucharist and the Sacrament of the Sick are also extraordinary spiritual tools in the process of healing. With Eucharist, we are strengthened for the journey with the bread of heaven. And with the Sacrament of the Sick, we are gently and mercifully blessed and anointed specifically for healing.

Healing does not depend on our faith; it depends on God's power. God chose to heal the centurion's servant, and he had no religious faith at all, but he did trust in the authority of Jesus. Jesus later remarked, "He had more trust than all of the Israelites."

Sacraments and prayer are very positive roads leading to healing. Even if miraculous healing does not occur, we have the healing presence of God in our midst, in our mind, in our memory.

One of my favorite quotes is by Bishop Sean O'Malley now Archbishop of Boston. When the gentle Capuchin Franciscan bishop was installed as bishop of the ailing Palm Beach Diocese (where its two previous bishops had resigned in shame), he said, "God never promised us a rose garden." He continued, "What God did promise us was that he would be with us until the end of time."

And it is this God of Presence that we seek in healing through prayer, sacraments, word, and community--a community of saints, both living and dead, a "cloud of witnesses" which surrounds us in our every moment, a blessed Mother who watches over us, and a God who never, never leaves our side. Emmanuel -- "God With Us."

> *"God never promised us a rose garden.*
> *". . . What God did promise us was that he would be with us until the end of time."*
> **Archbishop Sean O'Malley, OFM/Cap**

Reflection/Discussion Questions

1. Name some of the secondary losses you are experiencing. How are they affecting you?

_____

_____

_____

_____

_____

2. Are there important decisions that you should put off now? Are there decisions that you feel you can make comfortably?

_____

_____

_____

_____

_____

3. Are there tasks which you need to ask other people to help you with now? How do you feel about this? Will they be able to teach you how to do these tasks yourself when you are ready?

_____

_____

_____

_____

_____

4. What role do you miss most about your loved one?

_____

_____

_____

_____

_____

5. Have you taken advantage of community support such as hospice counseling, other counseling, other support groups? Can you recommend any to members of this group?

_____

_____

_____

_____

_____

6. Adjustment is a choice. Are you ready to make that choice? Or, do you need more time? What is the greatest challenge to your adjustment?

_____

_____

_____

_____

_____

7. How have your relationships with your faith community, your church, your pastor and staff been helpful to you? How can they be more helpful to you?

_____

_____

_____

_____

_____

8. What are some short-term goals you can make to help you "re-enter" or "re-organize" your life without your loved one?

_____

_____

_____

_____

Ponderings

What does the Church say about community?
"We believe in the communion of all the faithful of Christ, those who are pilgrims on earth, the dead who are being purified, and the blessed in heaven, all together forming one Church; and we believe that in this communion, the merciful love of God and his saints is always attentive to our prayers." *(Paul VI)*

Scripture Readings:
"They devoted themselves to the apostles' teaching and to the fellowship, to the breaking of bread and to prayer." *Acts 2:42*

"My command is this: Love each other as I have loved you."
John 15:12

Prayerful Suggestions:
1. The Sacrament of Reconciliation is available regularly here in our parish and in local parishes. We invite you to consider celebrating that healing sacrament.

2. If the Sacrament of the Sick is not offered regularly in your parish, speak with a priest about administering it to you during this time of intense grief.

3. The Sacrament of Eucharist is offered daily and on weekends here in our parish and in local parishes. Please come.

Practical Suggestions:
1. Ask a relative how they are doing. What can you do for them or others who are also grieving the loss of your loved one?

2. If there are other decisions which do not need to be made immediately, set a date in the future when you will think about these.

3. Take some time for yourself this week to "play." Go to a movie, or take a walk, or play golf, or go out to dinner with friends.

******VERY IMPORTANT Home Work: Visit one of the places where you and your loved one used to go or do something that you and your loved one used to do. Plan to share with the group at the next session. Add some more items to your Gratitude List.

Journaling

Date: _____

1. A significant event that occurred this week.
2. The person who was most important to me this week.
3. Changes I observe happening to me.
4. My plans for next week include . . .
5. Notes to myself . . .

_____
_____
_____
_____
_____
_____
_____
_____
_____
_____
_____
_____
_____
_____
_____
_____
_____
_____
_____
_____
_____
_____
_____
_____
_____
_____
_____
_____
_____
_____
_____
_____

Session Seven
REMEMBERING

Prayer: + In the name of the Father and of the Son and of the Holy Spirit. God of our creation, we bless you and praise you as we continue on our journey of life. In this time of remembering our loved ones, help us to remember the love of your son, Jesus Christ, and the power of His spirit among us. Wipe the tears from our eyes, as we pray in Jesus' most holy name. Amen.

Scripture: "This is my body to be given for you. Do this as a remembrance of me. (Jesus) did the same with the cup after eating, saying as he did so: "This cup is the new covenant in my blood, which will be shed for you." *Luke 22:19-20*

(Hymn will be played at end of session.)

Symbol:
    Our large empty plant container is now painted gold, inside and out and symbolizes the resurrection. The stone has been rolled away. Mary Magdalene ran all the way back to the Upper Room to tell the other disicples, "He is Risen! He is Risen!"
    The Lord has promised that he would go and prepare a place for us, Paradise. "In my Father's house, there are many mansions . . . I go to prepare a place for you."
    Even though we cannot see our loved one anymore or see what heaven really looks like, our symbol reminds us, "Eye cannot see, nor ear can hear the wonders that God has in store for those who love him."

The Last Supper

The celebration of Eucharist is the supreme remembrance of Christ. At the last supper with his disciples on the night before he died, he invited them to "do this in remembrance of me."

We honor Christ by remembering him every time we go to Mass and every time we receive Holy Communion.

Not only do we remember him, though; we gain strength, and peace, and grace from him in Communion. His memory assures us of life everlasting, of hope, of love, of peace, of Heaven where every tear will be wiped away.

Let us remember our own loved ones in a similar, but obviously not a sacramental, way. Let their memories be sources of strength to us; let us remember that they are also present to us now, though in a new way. Let their memories remind us of the cloud of witnesses who love us and support us as we go on down this road of adjustment, recovery, and new life. And, like our hymn says, "Let something of your heart and of your spirit be broken and shared with others."

Creative Responses

As we mentioned back in Session II, there are many ways to express and respond to our grief other than emotional responses. There are so many other positive expressions of grief.

Usually, people turn to their own best coping skills when other crises have occurred. Or, they turn to what they do best, which most certainly will appeal to the instrumental grievers among us.

Art, Poetry, Music, Hobbies

Eric Clapton wrote the song "Tears in Heaven" as he worked through the death of his small son. Other musicians, artists, and writers compose, paint, or write to express their grief. If you are a carpenter, build something that honors your loved one; if you are a gardener, design a garden or plant a special tree.

Reading/Research

People who love to read will turn to libraries for resources on grief management. More than 300 books have been written concerning the grieving process, varying from "For Children Who Have Lost a Loved One," to "For Those Who Are Divorced" to "Pet Loss" to "Handling the Holidays" to "Parents of Stillborns, Miscarriages, SIDS," to "Victims of Suicide, Murder, Other Violent Deaths", etc. Many of these books may be found in your local library.

Also, more academic resources are found on the Internet, which offers hundreds of informative articles on grief under the heading *www.grief.*

It is understood that many of you lack the concentration or ability to read and understand what you have read early on in the grieving process.

For many of you, though, who lean toward the instrumental griever end of the continuum, reading is one of the best forms of cognitive "grief work"

Memorial Acclamation

"We remember how you loved us to your death, and still we celebrate, for you are with us here; And we believe that we will see you when you come in your glory, Lord. We remember, we celebrate, we believe."

you can do for yourself. "Information seeking allows the griever to understand and validate one's responses and to assess possible strategies to adapt to the loss," (*Martin and Doka, 135.*)

Music

"The healing power of music is another source of revitalization for our damaged spirit," writes Elaine Stillwell in *The Death of A Child*. "The warm embrace of music's melody and words can make my heart feel like it is wrapped in velvet. It is my salvation on so many days."

Like this grieving mother (who lost two children in the same automobile accident, one four days after the other), I also find great warmth and love in remembering my children through songs such as "Daniel" by Elton John, "Danny Boy," "Forever Young," "The Rose," and many of my friend Fred Schott's songs. This is one of the reasons that I

"My Boy's Gone"

*You are still my boy even though
you're gone now.
We have your memory lingerin'on.
Boyish laughter rings out clear and it
seems you must be near.
Footsteps sound, and I look around
to see if you are here.*

*You still claim a part
of that hopeful place I call my heart.
Hopeless is a word I never learned.*

*My heart won't listen,
It just keeps missin'
that loving boy that it once knew.
You will always be,
You will always be,
Somewhere deep inside of me.*

*You are still my boy even though
you're gone now.
I hear your laughter lingerin' on.
I hear it; yes, it's true,
and no matter, no matter what I do,
no matter where I'm going to,
I'll always have my memories,
I'll always have my memories of you.*
*Harry Chapin
Cotton Patch Gospel*

---

have included his album in this program.

My favorite song for Debbie is "You Are My Sunshine," a song I sang over and over to her from the day she was born.

My most comforting song for Danny is one from "The Cotton Patch Gospel," by Harry Chapin entitled, "My Boy's Gone." In this down-home, blue-grass musical, the song tells of Mary and Josephs's feelings after Jesus has left home to fulfill his destiny.

Planning and Organizing

Cindy Lightner responded to her child's death, caused by a drunk driver, by founding Mothers Against Drunk Driving (MADD).

Similarly, the great attention given to missing children today grew from John Walsh's adaptive strategy for dealing with his son Adam's abduction and subsequent death.

On a less dramatic scale, mourners plan or participate in various events in honor or their loved ones or in fundraisers for charities which reflect the nature of their loved one's death. Our own son Danny is honored by the establishment of a scholarship for children less fortuate than he, and the planning and arranging for that scholarship fund allowed us to express our grief in a positive way.

Writing

As discussed earlier, there are many benefits to writing or journaling after a death. Some choose to write poetry; others simply write their feelings or find it helpful to record memories of their loved ones.

As it must be obvious to you by now, this project, "Harvesting Our Tears," has been a "life-saver" for me (a blended instrumental griever, by the way!) Researching the literature on death and dying, grief and bereavement, has been like a fresh breath of air for me in my understanding and mourning the loss of my two children.

This interest led me to the National Catholic Bereavement Ministry's national conference conveniently located in Ft. Lauderdale in 2004, where I heard excellent speakers in the field and made many contacts and new friends.

Later, I completed the training course offered by that group, and I am now nationally certified as a "Minister of Consolation."

Also, I have now joined our newly formed bereavement ministry in my own parish, where I have learned new skills in planning the funeral liturgy and made more new friends.

But, hopefully, the best news is yet to come: that "Harvesting Our Tears" will prove helpful to many others who are grieving their loved ones.

Photo Albums

After my daughter died, her father tediously sorted and arranged chronologically hundreds of photographs of Debbie from the time she was born until the day she died. This was an arduous task and one of the ways that he (a strongly instrumental griever) worked through some of his own grief. The result was a wonderful review of Debbie's life . . . in about seven albums!

Life Review

Less tedious, but just as helpful in healing, is to write a life review of your loved one. This does not have to be a biography geared for publication. It can be as simple as a brief outline of the person's life. You might ask other people to contribute to this life review by sharing their stories about your loved one.

> **"For those of us who are seeking the consolation of the Lord, we must seek first the Lord of consolation."**

Memory Quilt, Collages, Etc.

Another creative way to facilitate grieving is by making a "Memory Quilt" out of photos which have been scanned and transferred to fabric. This is a lovely gift for a small child remembering "Pop-Pop," for instance. Plus, it gives Grandma a marvelous project to help her work through her own grief.

Collages provide a creative means of telling one's life story. One idea is to create one on a 15" - 18" circle of cardboard and then frame it in a large embroidery hoop wrapped in ribbon. It makes a lovely wall decoration. In other words, "do your thing" in the grieving process.

In her book Elaine Stillwell mentions so many other ways to grieve such as "gardening, spending time at the beach, piano-playing, sewing, crocheting, stamp collecting, painting, cooking, studying a foreign language, making crafts, learning calligraphy, investigating digital photography, tracing genealogy, making furniture, baking bread, wallpapering, learning bird calls, painting portraits, studying opera, taking computer courses". . . an endless list!

Prayer is Healing

Prayer is good for you! Besides its efficacy, it provides a behavior for you that allows you to feel some control in a time when you feel you have no control. Pray novenas for strength, or consolation, or comfort. Spend time in church praying before the statues or the Stations of the Cross. The latter is an especially beneficial form of prayer as you contemplate the death of Jesus. In your grief, you also are experiencing the Paschal mystery . . . the suffering, death, and resurrection of Jesus. As painful as your suffering is now, it is comforting to meditate on the glories of the Resurrection.

And, of course, spend time asking the Blessed Mother's intervention.

Aside from their spiritual value, contemplative prayer and meditation are also very healthy forms of prayer in the focusing, centering, and breathing required in these forms.

Rituals

For special occasions, such as Thanksgiving, Christmas, your loved one's birthday, or the anniversary of the death, you may want to design your own ritual. It need not be complicated. It could be as simple as hanging a new ornament on the tree each year in memory of your loved one. Or, on the anniversary of the death, invite each member of the family to mention a memory that affirms your loved one. Plan a candlelight service.

A Remembrance Ritual

(*Note:* *Ideally, if a priest is available, Mass should be celebrated at the end of this session. If this is not possible, then please use this remembrance ritual.*)

Environment: If possible, move to another place. Place an open Bible next to a burning candle.

Presenter: On the night before he died, Our Lord, Jesus Christ asked us to remember him through a sacred meal of eating the bread and drinking the wine which was transformed into his body and his blood.

Today, we do not have the consecrated body and blood to use for Eucharist, but we can imagine that we have them in our minds. We will use these imaginary elements to memorialize and honor our loved ones as we honor Christ. This is called "The Practice of Creative Absence." The elements are absent and so are our loved ones, but we can bring them to mind in our memory as we remember them.

Prayer: +In the name of the Father and of the Son and of the Holy Spirit. Amen. Father of all gifts, Father of all memories, as we imagine these simple elements, help us to remember and honor our loved ones and our memories as gifts from you. And so we pray as we pray together before each meal,
> *"Bless us Oh Lord and these thy gifts*
> *which we are about to receive*
> *from thy bounty through Christ our Lord.*
> *Amen."*

(Invite each participant to place his/her plant in the center of the table near the candle as you read one of the phrases of the litany. The response is: " We honor and remember." They may add other phrases at the end of the litany, if they desire.)

1. For the many times we laughed together . . . We honor and remember..
2. For the many times we cried together . . . We honor and remember.
3. For the quiet times we shared . . .
4. For the disappointments we experienced . . .
5. For the times we forgot important dates --birthdays or anniversaries . . .
6. For the times we forgot to tell you how much we loved you . . .
7. For the wonderful times of celebration and accomplishment we shared . . .

8. For the millions of memories we shared . . .
9. For our favorite memory of you . . .
10. For the silly little things we did for each other . . .
(Other ...)

In the absense of the Body and the Blood, let us now in our minds imagine that we are receiving Holy Communion as a pledge, not only to remember Jesus, but as a pledge to remember and honor our absent loved ones, too. Keep in mind that Holy Communion is the sacred remembrance of Jesus Christ, as the Body and Blood are broken, poured out and shared. Let us listen now to the words of our hymn,as we imagine receiving Holy Communion.

Hymn Meditation: "Broken and Shared"
(For Sr. Mary Finn, HVM)

Refrain: **We want to have happen to us what happens to the bread. The bread becomes His body, broken and shared.**

We come to the word of our God. We come to the table of His body. We come because we have fellowship, with one another. He asks us to come because we are hungry for His word.

Put your life where the bread is. Let happen to your heart, let happen to your spirit what happens to the bread. Let something of your heart be broken by your brothers and yours sisters.

Let something of your spirit be broken and shared. Let something deep within you be poured out. We are bread and wine. We are His body on the earth.

You are my body, you are my blood. Go out to all my people, make them one. This is my command, to build the kingdom of your God.

Closing Prayer: Father God, when your son was close to his death, he asked that we all would eat the bread and drink the cup "in remembrance of Him." Help us to find ways to honor the memory of our loved one as we continue to move on with our lives. Grant us the grace and serenity to remember our loved ones and the legacies they left behind. We ask all of this in the name of the Father, and of the Son, and of the Holy Spirit. Amen.

Reflection Questions

1. Share your experience of going somewhere or doing something that reminded you greatly of your loved one.

_____
_____
_____
_____

2 Describe how you are expressing your grief. Has this choice changed over the past few weeks?

_____
_____
_____
_____

3. Name three major challenges resulting from your loss. What have you done about them? What would your loved one want you to do?

_____
_____
_____
_____

4. What are some small goals you can establish for yourself as you begin the adjustment to life without your loved one?

_____
_____
_____
_____

5.What hobbies/interests/talents could you return to or explore in order to find some refreshment and peace during this time of grief?

_____
_____
_____

6. If you could write an epitaph for your loved one, in a few words how would you describe him or her?

_____
_____
_____
_____

Ponderings . . .

What does the Church say?
"The Eucharist is the 'source and summit of the Christian life.' (LG 11) 'The other sacraments, and indeed all ecclesiastical ministries and works of the apostolate, are bound up with the Eucharist and are oriented toward it. For in the blessed Eucharist is contained the whole spiritual good of the Church, namely Christ himself, our Pasch' (PO 5)" *(CCC1324).*

Scripture: "I am the bread of life. He who comes to me will never go hungry, and he who believes in me will never be thirsty" *(John 6:35).*

Practical Suggestions:
1. Think ahead to an important day in your life that is coming next (a holiday, your loved one's birthday, anniversary of death.) Plan a ritual to celebrate and remember your loved one on that day, even if you only celebrate it yourself.

2. Choose to express your grief differently. Try something new, or renew an old goal, interest or hobby.

3. Add favorite memories of your loved one to your "Gratitude List."

Prayerful Suggestions:
1. We suggest that each person ponder the words of our hymn for this session *"Broken and Shared"* just before the next time they go to Mass. "We want to have happen to us what happens to the bread . . ."

Food for Thought:
"There is only one thing worse than speaking ill of the dead, and that is not speaking about the dead." -- *Anonymous*

Homework for Session #8: None.

Journaling

1. A significant event that occurred this week.
2. The person who was most important to me this week.
3. Changes I observe happening to me.
4. My plans for next week include . . .
5. Notes to myself . . .

_____

_____

_____

_____

_____

_____

_____

_____

_____

_____

_____

_____

_____

_____

_____

_____

_____

_____

_____

_____

_____

_____

_____

_____

Session Eight
"MOVING ON"

Prayer: Father, Creator of all good gifts, we thank you and praise you for your patience with us as we traveled these roads together during the past eight weeks. We thank you for the new friends we have made, for the new insights we have received, and most of all for helping us to come to a new place with our loved one deep in our heart and memory. Bless all those who mourn. Bless all those who are just beginning this journey. Bless all who will come behind us. We pray in the name of the Father and of the Son and of the Holy Spirit. Amen.

Scripture: "The LORD is the eternal God,
creator of the ends of the earth.
. . . They that hope in the LORD will renew their strength,
they will soar as with eagles' wings.
They will run and not grow weary,
walk and not grow faint." *(Is. 40: 28, 31)*

Meditation Hymn: **"Fly Like an Eagle"**
(In loving memory of my father, Francis X. Schott, Sr.)

Refrain: **You will fly like an eagle. In my love you will soar.**
On my hand I will raise you to your home in my love.

You who hold God for your strength
and make your home in the shadow of his wings,
say to him: You are my refuge; in God I trust.

The Lord will keep you from harm and those who would destroy you.
Let his wings be your shelter.
Trust in the Lord; He is your shield.

My angels shall be with you all the days of your life.
In their hands is your safety.
You shall not stumble, you shall not fall.

Those who call in my name,
I shall always be with them, giving peace, giving joy.
The life that I give will be forever.

Symbol: *The golden container now holds the actual remnants of the old plant, the old life of your loved one, but now changed (re-rooted) into new life. What better symbolism could we have of the funeral directive, "Life has not ended; life has changed." and that refers to our own lives, as well.*

"You have turned my mourning into dancing; you have taken off my sackcloth and clothed me with joy, so that my soul may praise you and not be silent."
                                    Psalm 30:11.

"I give you thanks, O Lord, with my whole heart . . . On the day I called, you answered me, you increased my strength of soul."
                                    Psalm 138:1,3

SUMMARY

Over these past seven weeks, we have discussed the nature of grief, various grieving patterns, death and suffering, our brokenness, the need for forgiveness, family and community as support systems, and remembering and honoring our loved ones.

The purpose of this last session is to help you move on to the next steps of grieving. Some grief management programs have a closing celebration at the end of the last session which signifies "Graduation," implying we have finished grieving.

We, too, will have a closing celebration, but it will be a "Going Forth" ceremony, a ceremony which will not imply that our grieving is over but will encourage us to move on to continue the process.

Where We've Been

We have been working on the four major tasks to be achieved in the grieving process, according to Dr. J. William Worden in his book *Grief Counseling and Grief Therapy.*

1. **To accept the reality of the loss.**
2. **To experience the pain of grief.**
3. **To adjust to an environment in which the deceased is missing.**
4. **To "emotionally relocate" the deceased and move on with life.**

If you have worked through the first seven sessions of this program, you are probably well past the first two tasks and either "adjusting to an environment where your loved one is missing" or beginning the fourth task of "emotionally relocating" your loved one and moving on with your life.

We all know too well by now that life does not stop with the loss of our loved one. In fact, there are times when we are amazed that life goes on so normally with people driving their cars, going to work, taking children to school, going to the grocery store, playing golf or bowling . . . and we think to ourselves, "How can they be so normal? Don't they know that my loved one is gone?"

Toward the end of his life, Robert Frost was asked to sum up everything he had learned about life. His reply was, "In three words I can sum up everything I've learned about life: *it goes on*."

The bills need paid, cooking and preparing meals are still necessary. If you are employed, you still must get up every morning and go to work. If you're not, you must find meaningful activities to fill the days of loneliness and grief.

Where You've Been

Think back to the time immediately after the loss of your loved one. How have your feelings and thoughts changed? You are at a point of arrival now, as you review the past weeks and months of living without your loved one. You also are at a point of departure as you envision even more changes ahead.

You will never, never forget your loved one, but you will find that you are not thinking constantly of him or her. Little things no longer lead to a meltdown of tears. You delight in hearing stories that recall your loved one fondly. You feel better. You don't hurt as much. You, who entered "no man's land" when you lost your loved one, are now standing on more familiar turf and you are managing. You are coping, and you are becoming much more confident in moving on.

You will begin to experience your loved one in "a different place." This is what is meant by "emotionally relocating" your loved one to a special place in your heart. You will have a totally different relationship than when he or she was alive, but, nevertheless, a valid relationship. You are joined together with your loved one spiritually.

You may find yourself communicating with your loved one. This is not at all unusual. Sometimes, you speak to them, and sometimes they may answer you in your heart. Sometimes, you may feel that you actually experience them in the flesh, in an experience that is so real that you will swear that they were actually at your side. Other times, you may experience them in your dreams. No, you are not crazy! These experiences are real to you. Consider them blessings. Some people never experience these consolations. You are blessed.

Where You're Going

As a believing Christian, one of

the greatest consolations is to have the *assurance* that you will eventually be going to Paradise when you die and your loved ones will be there waiting for you. If you have ever read any of the research concerning "near-death" or "life-after-death" experiences, you will know that these experiences are all pretty much the same. As these people are leaving their bodies, they see a tunnel with a very bright light beckoning them. Many of their loved ones are there, awaiting them, welcoming them to "the other side."

Meanwhile, you are continuing the grief process. You choose to honor your loved one by living as rich and full a life as possible under your particular circumstances. People question the length of time it takes to finish the grieving process. Of course, it is different for each person, but most of the experts agree that many people take at least two to five years to go through the whole process. Grief is a long-term process; the good news is that it doesn't hurt as much as it did in the beginning.

Remember, you are not alone in your grief.

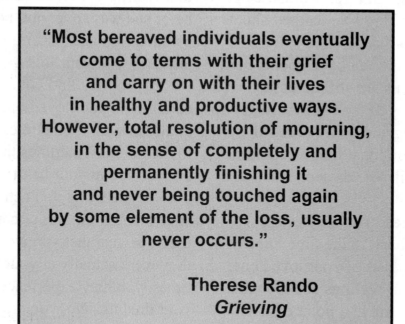

"Most bereaved individuals eventually
come to terms with their grief
and carry on with their lives
in healthy and productive ways.
However, total resolution of mourning,
in the sense of completely and
permanently finishing it
and never being touched again
by some element of the loss, usually
never occurs."

Therese Rando
Grieving

Am I Making Progress?

Elaine E. Stillwell, M.A., M.S.
Rockville Centre, NY

Since I lost my two oldest children, 19 year old Peggy and 21 year old Denis, in the same automobile accident, I found it helpful to assess the status of my grief every so often, checking to see if I was on the right mind-track for mending my fragile, hurting heart. Do yourself a favor and see if you have any areas of the heart that need nurturing. the following "check list" will help you set some goals for feeling better.

Allow Yourself:
Time to cry
Space to think
To remember your loved one
Realistic goals
To do whatever gives you
a moment's peace
To be imperfect
To accept offers of help
To pamper yourself

Force Yourself:
To do old routines
To listen to your family
To do an activity that you
used to do

Convince Yourself:
That each person grieves
differently
That you will get better

Let Yourself:
Off the hook
Laugh
Feel anger
Tell God how you honestly feel
Treasure a special friend
Remember happy memories
Select what you can handle
"Wear-out" feelings of anger,
guilt and depression

Teach Yourself:
To take care of yourself
To learn everything about
the grief process
To set goals
To turn to life
To ignore hurtful comments of
others

Talk to yourself:
About anything
About how your loved one
would like you to
handle things
Have a dialogue with your
loved one

Forgive Yourself:
We make mistakes
We're not perfect
Our loved ones weren't perfect
They know they were loved

Find Yourself:
*(We become different people
with different needs.)*
Through meditation
Through reading
Through singing
Through writing
Through talking
Through new friends
Through new hobbies

Indulge Yourself:
Shop
Nap
Walk
Daydream
Say "I deserve that!"
Set aside special time for
yourself
Don't rush or overwhelm
yourself with activities

Express Yourself:
Tell the story of your loved one
Tell the world how you feel
Tell your family how you
really feel
Try new activities
Find new ways to "reinvest"
that special love you
shared with your
loved one

Forget Yourself:
Seek out other bereaved
persons
Talk to them
Share what you've
learned -- what's
given you moments
of peace. You'll find
"helping is healing."

Give Yourself:
No deadlines
Choose to rebuild your life in a
meaningful way
Keep memories of your
loved one alive
Make your loved one
proud of you

*Get busy taking care of yourself
and may your efforts bring
peace and joy to your heart.* --
Elaine E. Stillwell

(Elaine is Founder and Chapter Leader of The Compassionate Friends of Rockville, NY; the Coordinator for the Bereaved, Separated and Divorced in the Diocese of Rockville Centre; and a former Board Member of the National Catholic Ministry to the Bereaved.)

What Recovery Means

Following is a list of items which indicate a high degree of recovery. The first seven are suggesed by John James and Frank Cherry in *The Grief Recovery Handbook*. The remaining ones have been gathered from other sources and are listed by Stanley Cornils in *Your Healing Journey Through Grief*.

1. *You are feeling better.*
2. *You are managing your grief through self-direction.*
3. *You find new meaning for living without the fear of future abandonment.*
4. *You are able to enjoy fond memories without having them bring painful feelings.*
5. *You can acknowledge that it is okay to feel bad from time to time.*
6. *You are able to forgive others when they say or do things that you know are based on their lack of knowledge about grief.*
7. *Your ability to talk about your loss is in fact helping another person to get through his or her loss.*
8. *You will also find new opportunities and priorities which you formerly overlooked.*
9. *You have become aware again of the loved ones you still have.*
10. *You are committing yourself to living more fully and meaningfully.*
11. *You are gaining a new and increased awareness of the precariousness of life and its brevity.*
12. *You are learning not to put off the important things you can say and do today.*
13. *You have become aware of any unfinished business in your life.*
14. *You are enjoying an increased family commitment and unity.*
15. *You have developed a greater personal growth and an increased interest in spiritual things.*
16. *When you imagine that the person you have lost seems to be moving farther into your memory, it's a sign that you have been climbing the steps of mourning successfully.*

What Recovery Does *Not* Mean

Stanley Cornils in *Your Healing Journey Through Grief* offers this list with the caveat that total resolution of grief is a false goal and usually does not occur.

Recovery does *not* mean:

1. You will forget your loved one.
2. You will no longer have a relationship with your loved one.
3. You are always going to be happy and never experience pain.
4. You will not experience the bittersweet combination of feelings that holidays bring.
5. You will not be touched by certain reminders, songs, smells, special locations.
6. You will not painfully wish that your lost one is present at important events or milestones.
7. You will not mourn any more, but you will not mourn acutely.

REFLECTION QUESTIONS

1. How have your thoughts, behavior, and feelings changed since the day you lost your loved one?

_____
_____
_____
_____
_____

2. Have you discovered growth or adjustments which you never dreamed were possible?

_____
_____
_____
_____
_____

3. What do you have to say to the group now? Can you see changes in any of them since the group started meeting?

_____
_____
_____
_____
_____

4. Name some short-term goals and long-term goals for the future.

_____
_____
_____
_____
_____
_____

5. How would you feel about having a group reunion three months from now? If group agrees, set date: _____

Ponderings . . .

"Those who sow in tears
will reap with songs of joy.
He who goes out weeping,
carrying seed to sow,
will return with songs of joy,
carrying sheaves with him" *(Ps. 126: 5-6).*

Practical Suggestions:

1. List the "sheaves" you will be carrying after harvesting your tears.
2. During this grieving process and as it continues, are you touching peoples' lives with goodness, with faith, with charity?
3. If you have not yet done so, please consider volunteering for a charity of your choice, perhaps one connected with your loved one's death (American Cancer Society, American Heart Society, Alzheimer's, and so forth.)

Prayerful Suggestions:

1. Continue your gratitude list forever and get it out and read it whenever you are feeling blue.
2. Begin each day with a morning prayer such as, "Lord, there is nothing that can happen today that you and I can't handle together." Or, "Lord, open my eyes so I do not miss the grace of this day!"
3. Reach out to someone who has lost a loved one recently. Be there for them.

Food for Thought: "There is nothing permanent except change."   *Heraclitus*

"In three words I can sum up everything I've learned about life: *it goes on."*
Robert Frost

"Although the world is full of suffering, it is also full of overcoming it."
Helen Keller

"Those who don't know how to weep with their whole heart don't know how to laugh either."   *Golda Meir*

Homework: Be at peace.   "Soar like an eagle . . ." "Run the good race. . ." "Run like a deer . . ." "Walk in faith . . ."   "Go!"

Journaling

Date: _____

1. A significant event that occurred this week.
2. The person who was most important to me this week.
3. Changes I observe happening to me.
4. My plans for next week include . . .
5. Notes to myself . . .

_____

_____

_____

_____

_____

_____

_____

_____

_____

_____

_____

_____

_____

_____

_____

_____

_____

_____

_____

_____

_____

_____

_____

_____

_____

_____

APPENDIX A

What Type of Griever Are You?

"I don't seem to get as upset as most other people I know."
"I seem to get so much more upset than most people I know."
"I avoid highly emotional situations."
"Every situation is emotional for me."
"I sometimes feel guilty for not having more intense feelings."
"I can't stop my grieving by thinking of other things."
"I resent efforts to get me to show feelings that I don't have."
"I resent efforts to get me to stop showing my feelings."
"My friends think I am avoiding my grief."

Do any of these statements apply to you? If so, this article is for you!

Conventional Theory

Conventional bereavement theory tells us that "Unless we name and address and feel and work through all of our feelings, we will 'crash, become ill, break down -- either physically, mentally or emotionally'-- either sooner or later." Nearly every expert in the field of bereavement says basically the same thing. However, they still caveat their theory with the generalized caution . . . "Everyone grieves in his or her own way" . . .

Time after time I see examples in the literature of men (mostly) who do not follow the conventional pattern of grieving and thus are "worried about" by other family members and friends.

Good friends of these "non-grievers" who grieve unconventionally say things like, "Steve is still in denial," "Joe seems to be too happy," "What's the matter with Leo . . . didn't he love Elizabeth as much as we thought he did?"

In the instance of parents losing a child, case after case also points to the differences between a mother's and father's grieving behaviors, which may be a likely factor in the resulting high percentage of separation or divorce after the death of a child. "Poor John or Dick or Art . . . he just can't let his hair down and show his true feelings."

Often, in these cases, the "true feelings" are not as intense as those of others, especially women, and therefore are not "acceptable."

Their grief, while still as intense a *protest* against their loss as we have defined it earlier, is not validated as authentic grief.

Other people do not understand that their grief is just as deep and just as severe; it's just that many people, mostly men, do not express their protest/grief in ways that are similar to the more "acceptable" forms of affective expression such as crying, sobbing, sighing, sharing their feelings with others, or seeking help through counseling or support groups.

Nonconventional Theory

How delighted I was when I heard Dr. Kenneth Doka speak about gender-based stereotypes of grief at a national conference on bereavement. He and his partner, Dr. Terry L. Martin have described their groundbreaking research in **Men Don't Cry; Women Do: Transcending Gender Stereotypes of Grief** in Philadelphia publisher Brunner/ Mazel's Series in Death, Dying and Bereavement.

Dr. Martin is an Assistant Professor of Psychology at Hood College in Frederick, Maryland and a licensed clinical psychologist specializing in death-related issues who has taught both undergraduate and graduate courses in thanatology for more than twenty years.

Dr. Doka is a Professor of Gerontology at the Graduate School of the College of New Rochelle in New York, Senior Consultant to the Hospice Foundation of America, and the author of seventeen books on death and dying.

The authors theorize that grief patterns can be divided into two specific groupings, identified as **"Intuitive Grieving"** and **"Instrumental Grieving."** (At first they called these feminine and masculine grieving patterns, but changed them to the present names since they found that many women may be instrumental grievers and many men may demonstrate characteristics of intuitive grieving. Both men

and women also may be what the authors identify as "blended balanced grievers," expressing their grief equally in intuitive and instrumental behaviors.

Theory Supported

Perhaps the highly respected conventional theorist Therese Rando validates their theory best, writing, in the Foreword of their book, "Martin and Doka have challenged traditionally held, yet empirically unsupported, notions that have caused varying levels of harm to a significant proportion of bereaved individuals and to their loved ones."

She acknowledges, "One of the many strengths of this book is the explicit identification of the general Western bias in mental health that affective (emotional) expression is necessary for healthy grief and mourning. While this supports the intuitive griever, it actually can hurt the instrumental griever. One need observe just one instance where the counselor engages in a power struggle to wrest tears from an instrumental mourner, in a mistaken belief that only through such expression will that person be able to effectively contend with their loss, to appreciate the countertherapeutic, and often iatrogenic, effects such a myth can have." *(Webster defines iatrogenic as*

"imagined symptoms, ailments, or disorders induced by a physician's words . . .")
Rando continues, "Two corollaries stem from this widespread but mistaken belief. The first, the 'grief work hypothesis,' asserts that it is only by experiencing strong affect (emotion) and working it through that loss can be accommodated.

"The second corollary is that the absence of affective expression suggests some type of pathological response."

Monumental Findings

Doka and Martin, using their theoretical framework as a way of interpreting existing research, showed that many people grieve differently than previously thought. Rather than grieve in the affective (emotional) realm common to intuitive grievers, the responses of the instrumental grievers to the protest within are often outwardly expressed in other modalities such as cognitive (thinking), physical (doing) and spiritual (understanding) response tendencies. These findings, which Dr. Doka refers to as "empirically supported theory," have proven monumental in the field of bereavement management where for all these years most of the foundational information concerned the death itself.

Blended Grievers

There are very few purely 100% instrumental grievers, or many 100% intuitive grievers. Instead, Martin and Doka found that there is a continuum where most of the grievers are found, either as profoundly or moderately one type of griever with many more "blended grievers" having some characteristics of the other type. Additionally, there are "blended balanced" types of grievers, where their expressions of grief are nearly equally balanced between the two types of grievers.

There is a third group of grievers that Doka and Martin identify: dissonant grievers. These are people who are feeling one way and acting another. A good example is a person with conflicted ideas of how they *should* behave, based on the expectations of others or themselves or of unusual circumstances.

What Kind Of Griever Am I?

Speaking personally, I myself had wondered about my own grieving style or pattern. While I certainly was expressing my grief affectively through an outpouring of tears and sobbing after the deaths of both children, I also eventually found myself doing mundane housework, redecorating the family room and porch (which involved lots of painting and sewing) and, finally, supervising the remodeling of our kitchen. Also, I found myself spending a great deal of time reading everything I could get my hands on concerning the grieving process, and when I could not locate a Catholic faith-based support group, I began to design and develop this one for the Church.

So, by all counts, I was not just affectively grieving. However, I was feeling guilty and concerned that I was using these activities to deny or avoid my grief. I considered my "escape" outlets as something abnormal (and almost shameful) until I read Doka and Martin's helpful book.

I was so relieved to find that, according to their theory, I am a "blended griever," leaning toward the intuitive grieving side of the continuum. I was expressing my grief (particularly my *protest* against the totally unexpected death of a second child, Debbie) through physical behaviors (cleaning, painting and sewing), cognitive behaviors (reading and planning, designing, and developing a new grief process), and spiritually (seeking understanding, questioning God, and seeking a spiritual director to help me sort things out about my faith.)

What Kind Of Griever Are You?

Take a few moments now to respond to the twenty-five statements in the **Grief Pattern Inventory** which follows on the next three pages. Just follow the instructions and then self-score your answers, according to the instructions for scoring.

Gratitude

So, for our purposes here, we will attempt early in this process to identify the types of grievers who are participating in the "Harvesting Our Tears" process. Each session will suggest activities for both the intuitive and instrumental grievers, also encouraging those "blended grievers" to adapt these activities.

To Dr. Martin and Dr. Doka, "Thank you for the new information you have contributed to the field. Personally, I am grateful for the gifts you have given me -- relief, understanding and and sanity!"

Men Don't Cry; Women Do by Dr. Terry Martin and Dr. Kenneth Doka, published by Brunner/Mazel, a subdivision of Taylor & Francis Group, 325 Chestnut Street, Philadelphia, PA 19106. It also is available from Amazon.com   .

GRIEF PATTERN INVENTORY

Please respond to each of the following statements using the key below. If appropriate, circle the response that best describes you in the past 2 weeks.

A=Always,   U=Usually,   S= Sometimes,   R=Rarely,   N=Never

1. A U S R N   I am more emotional than most people I know.

2. A U S R N   It is easy for me to cry and show my feelings to others.

3. A U S R N   Even though I have returned to my normal routine, I still have strong and painful feelings about my loss.

4. A U S R N   Even though I feel like crying, I do not cry in front of others.

5. A U S R N   Although I am grieving in my own way, others may think me cold and unfeeling.

6. A U S R N   I don't seem to get as upset as most other people I know.

7. A U S R N   I feel overwhelmed by feelings of grief.

8. A U S R N   I appreciate when others encourage me to share my painful feelings with them.

9. A U S R N   I avoid highly emotional or "touchy-feely" situations of any kind.

10. A U S R N   It is important to me that others view me as being in control.

11. A U S R N   I have been told that I am avoiding my grief even though I don't think that I am.

12. A U S R N   I have been controlling my painful feelings by drinking or by using other prescription or nonprescription drugs.

13. A U S R N   I believe that a bereavement support group is (would be) very helpful for me.

14. A U S R N   I worry that I am not as upset by my loss as I should be, and feel guilty that I don't have more intense feelings.

86

15. A U S R N   I resent efforts to get me to show feelings that I don't have.

16. A U S R N   I think more about my loss than feel things about my loss.

17. A U S R N   I believe it is very important to be aware of, and in touch with, all of my feelings.

18. A U S R N   I find that solving problems associated with my loss helps me.

19. A U S R N   Although I can sometimes control my painful feelings, they usually return and overwhelm me.

20. A U S R N   Since my loss, I feel like I'm just pretending to be strong in front of most people.

21. A U S R N   I find that I can't stop my grieving by thinking of other things.

22. A U S R N   I have taken deliberate action to honor the memory of my loved one, even though I have not been as upset as most others who are grieving my loved one.

23. A U S R N   Others seem surprised by my recovery from my loss.

24. A U S R N   Although I took care of things immediately after my loved one's death, I was surprised when I eventually "crashed" and began to have intense and painful feelings.

25. A U S R N   I would describe myself as more intellectual than emotional.

SCORING

Please total your scores for the three groups of questions, according to the following scale:

A = + 2   U = +1   S = 0   R = -1   N = -2

Group A Question #		Group B Question #		Group C Question #	
1	___	5	___	4	___
2	___	6	___	10	___
3	___	9	___	12	___
7	___	11	___	14	___
8	___	15	___	20	___
13	___	16	___		
17	___	18	___		
19	___	21	___		
22	___	23	___		
24	___	25	___		

Group A Total Score: _____

16 - 20 Profoundly intuitive pattern
11 - 15 Moderate intuitive pattern
 6 - 10 Blended intuitive pattern
-5 - +5 Blended balanced patterns

Group B Total Score: _____

16 - 20 Profoundly instrumental pattern
11 - 15 Moderate instrumental pattern
 6- 10 Blended instrumental pattern
-5 - +5 Blended balanced patterns

Group C:
If an individual item score is either +1 or +2, it is a "dissonant response."
Each dissonant response should be evaluated separately.

Continuum

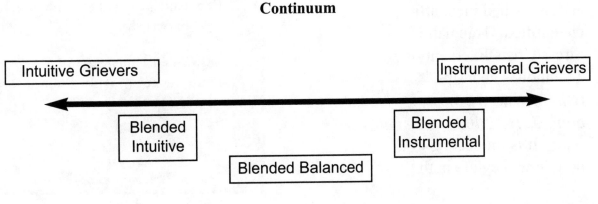

88

APPENDIX B

The Grief Process and Trauma

These seven phases are the seven stages of the grief process involved with a major traumatic event such as the terrorist

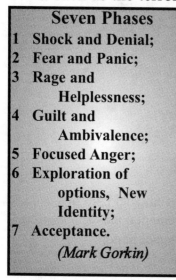

Seven Phases

1. Shock and Denial;
2. Fear and Panic;
3. Rage and Helplessness;
4. Guilt and Ambivalence;
5. Focused Anger;
6. Exploration of options, New Identity;
7. Acceptance.

(Mark Gorkin)

attacks of Septemember 11th identified and described by Mark Gorkin, MSW, LICSW, and published in an article entitled "Traumatic Stress/Crisis Intervention Techniques and Tips," (*Businessknow how. com, July, 2002.*) It is interesting to note how they are both

similar to and different from the classic stages of grief described by three experts in the field of bereavement management.

Four Tasks of Mourning

1. To accept the reality of the loss.
2. To experience the pain of grief.
3. To adjust to an environment in which the deceased is missing.
4. To "emotionally relocate" the deceased and move on with life.

William Worden, Ph.D.

Five Stages of Grief

1. Denial
2. Anger
3. Bargaining
4. Depression
5. Acceptance

Elizabeth Kubler Ross

Six "R's" of Grief

1. Recognizing the loss.
2. Reacting to the separation.
3. Recollecting and re-experiencing the deceased and the relationship.
4. Relinquishing the old attachments to the deceased.
5. Readjusting to move adaptively into the new world without forgetting the old.
6. Reinvesting in new relationships.

(Therese Rando)

"TEARS" SCRIPTURE

Record my lament:
List my tears on your scroll--
are they not in the record?
Psalm 56:9

You changed my wailing into dancing;
You removed my sackcloth and clothed me with joy,
That my soul may sing to you and not be silent.
O LORD my God,I will give you thanks forever.
Ps. 30: 11

You have fed them with the bread of tears;
you have made them drink tears by the bowlful.
Restore us, O God almighty;
make your face shine upon us, that we may be saved.
Psalm 80:5

Those who sow in tears
will reap with songs of joy.
He who goes out weeping,
carrying seed to sow,
will return with songs of joy,
carrying sheaves with him
(Ps. 126: 5-6).

On this mountain...he will destroy the shroud that enfolds all peoples,
the sheet that covers all nations;
he will swallow up death forever.
The Sovereign LORD will wipe away the tears from all faces.
Isaiah 25:6

She brought an alabaster jar of perfume,
and as she stood behind him at his feet weeping,
she began to wet his feet with her tears.
Then she wiped them with her hair,
kissed them and poured perfume on them.
Luke7:38

For the Lamb at the center of the throne
will be their shepherd;
he will lead them to springs of living water.
And God will wipe away every tear from their eyes.
Rev. 7: 17

Bibliography

Cornils, Stanley (2003). *Your healing journey through grief: a practical approach to grief management*. San Francisco: Reed Publishers

Del Zoppo, Patrick. (1995). *Mourning: the journey from grief to healing.* New York:Alba House.

Kushner, Harold. (1981). *When bad things happen to good people.* New York:,HarperCollins.

O'Brien, Mauryeen, (2000). *The* new day journal, rev. ed. Chicago: ACTA.

Martin, Terry. and Doka, Kenneth., (2000). *Men don't cry . . . .women do.* New York: Taylor and Francis.

Rando, Therese. (1988). *How to go on living when someone you love dies.* New York: Bantam Books.

Schiff, Harriet S. (1977). *The bereaved parent.* New York: Penguin.

Stillwell, Elaine E. (2004). *The death of a child: reflections for grieving parents.* Chicago: ACTA.

Worden, William (1991). *Grief counseling and grief therapy: a handbook of the mental health practiitioner (2nd ed.)* New York: Springer.

O God, when all is in darkness
and we feel our weakness
and helplessness,
give us the sense of your presence,
your love and your strength.

Help us to have perfect trust
in your protecting love
and strengthening power,
so that nothing may frighten or worry us.

Living close to you,
we shall see your hand,
your purpose, your will
through all things.

. . . St. Ignatius of Loyola

Gratitude List

Please take a few minutes each day and write down five things you are grateful for. Add five more each day. You will be surprised. Keep this list near you when you are "blue."

(Gratitude List, continued)

For Additional Copies

Sold Separately (or in quantities less than 10): $18 per manual/CD*
    The cost of a 95-page (8 1/2 x 11") manual and CD (attached to the inside back cover of the manual) is $18per participant. The **Facilitator's Guide** is $5.

Parish Packet: 10 or more - $15 per manual/CD

(For prices of similar manuals, please see   www.mournerspath. com).

*Plus shipping and handling.

ORDER DIRECTLY FROM
JEREMIAH PRESS
FAX: 561-368-~~2322~~ 2207
OR
JEREMIAHPR@AOL.COM
OR
www.jeremiahpress.com

**Also, please see Jeremiah Press for additional
parish programs.**